PULL UP YOUR YOUR C.H.A.I.R.

CICELY SIMPSON

PULL UP YOUR C.H.A.I.R.

FIVE STRATEGIES TO **CHANGE THE TRAJECTORY** OF YOUR CAREER

ForbesBooks

Published by ForbesBooks, Charleston, South Carolina.
Member of Advantage Media Group.

ForbesBooks is a registered trademark, and the ForbesBooks colophon is a trademark of Forbes Media, LLC.

Printed in the United States of America.

10 9 8 7 6 5 4 3 2 1

ISBN: 978-1-95588-416-7
LCCN: 2021923234

Cover and layout design by David Taylor.

This custom publication is intended to provide accurate information and the opinions of the author in regard to the subject matter covered. It is sold with the understanding that the publisher, Advantage|ForbesBooks, is not engaged in rendering legal, financial, or professional services of any kind. If legal advice or other expert assistance is required, the reader is advised to seek the services of a competent professional.

 Advantage Media Group is proud to be a part of the Tree Neutral® program. Tree Neutral offsets the number of trees consumed in the production and printing of this book by taking proactive steps such as planting trees in direct proportion to the number of trees used to print books. To learn more about Tree Neutral, please visit **www.treeneutral.com**.

Since 1917, Forbes has remained steadfast in its mission to serve as the defining voice of entrepreneurial capitalism. ForbesBooks, launched in 2016 through a partnership with Advantage Media Group, furthers that aim by helping business and thought leaders bring their stories, passion, and knowledge to the forefront in custom books. Opinions expressed by ForbesBooks authors are their own. To be considered for publication, please visit **www.forbesbooks.com**.

This book is dedicated to …

My father, James Simpson
Corporal, United States Marine Corps
Vietnam Veteran
June 16, 1947, to April 12, 2020

My mother, Pat Simpson,
who always encourages me to take leaps
of faith in life, saying, "Just pray."

My brother, Shawn Simpson,
who is my rock. No words can express my
sincere gratitude to and for him.

Kelly Simpson and Jordan Simpson,
for their enduring support.

CONTENTS

ACKNOWLEDGMENTS

The most important acknowledgment is my faith in Jesus Christ. Every door that opens and every door that closes is God showing me a different path. I would never have guessed my career would be in business and politics. Even if you are not a person of faith, believe that there is something greater than you leading and directing your path.

I am thankful for the individuals who have shaped my leadership journey and believed in me over the past twenty-five-plus years: Amy Dement, Jan Cyr, Gail Norwood, Phyllis Menees, Bernie James, Connie James, Janet Kerr, Chuck Cagle, Beecher Frasier, US Congressman Lincoln Davis, US Congressman Jim Cooper, AJ Jones, Robert Primus, Justin Maierhofer, Vickie Walling, Chuck Merin, Steve Caldeira, Karen Raskopf, Nigel Travis, Chrissy Pace, Matthew Lopes, Jessica Falborn, Montee Wynn, and Dr. Adetola Kassim. These individuals, and so many others, have informed the leadership strategies and lessons that are captured in this book.

Ilene Rein and Chris Prouty: This book would not have happened without you. I'm humbled by your friendship and support.

I am grateful for my lobbying clients who trust me every day to represent them in the halls of power in Washington, DC.

I am also grateful and thankful for my coaching clients, who allow me to walk alongside them on their leadership journey. Thank you for trusting me to coach your career transformation to achieve the success you desire.

Last but certainly not least is the Advantage Media team: Harper, Jake, Bree, Kristin, Simon, Rusty, Rachel, Laura, Courtney, Isabelle, Miguel, Joe, Lyka, Ben, Lexi, and David. Thank you for making my dream to write a book a reality.

TAKING A SEAT AT THE TABLE

In 2020, I was asked to be a guest speaker at a leadership seminar, talking to an audience of CEOs and executives. As I approached this speech, I wanted to come up with a new way to tell people what I've done and how I've done it. While preparing for my presentation, I came across a quote from Shirley Chisholm, the first African American woman in Congress, who said, "If they don't give you a seat at the table, bring a folding chair."

That was it! That brilliant statement summed up the way I've lived my life, and will continue to do so. When I shared the quote with my audience, people immediately wrote it down. I went on to explain that I often needed to "bring my own chair" and "make my way" to job interviews, to meetings, to … you name it!

After my presentation, I pondered Shirley Chisholm's quote for days. The more I used the quote, the more it captured people's attention, and the feedback was instantaneous. In fact, it became so popular that I developed the C.H.A.I.R. Leadership program. I am now on a mission to help you with tips and strategies that will change the trajectory of your career and your life.

While I did not know it at the time, the genesis for my leadership program—and this book—started in my childhood. My father was a Marine, a Vietnam veteran. As you can imagine, discipline and execution were the order of the day! He believed that all of us make our own paths in life, and we must take responsibility for ourselves and our actions. I always remember him as being firm but kind. He had a teacher's heart and would use any circumstance or situation to help my brother and me understand how life works *for* us—when we decide to take responsibility.

For example, if my father needed a car repaired, he would have my brother or me make the call. If he needed to make a doctor's appointment, one of us would call the office. If there was a problem with a utility bill—you guessed it—my brother or I would be handed the phone. Now, you may be thinking, *Why would he be mean enough to have his kids make these calls?*

Unbeknownst to my brother and me, my father had a logical and long-term reasoning for having us do this. He was standing right beside us, listening to the call, giving us directions to follow. He would say things like, "Okay, now say … Now ask …" My father did this with us well into our teen years, and by that time we were used to having conversations and articulating beyond our age. We learned to know what we were saying, why we were saying it, and how to say it clearly to communicate our message. When I look back, I can see he was teaching us how to create conversations, to *champion* ourselves, to be *honest* with ourselves and others, and to have a positive *impact* on others.

Without realizing it, my father was coaching my brother and me. He was instilling principles and values that would make us successful.

My father challenged and motivated us to work harder than everyone else—to go the extra mile to accomplish our goals. My education is a great example. I enjoyed school, but tests and exams were a challenge. One day, I came home beaming because I received a ninety-eight on a test. I was so proud of myself and just knew my dad would be too. However, after he reviewed my test, he asked, "Why wasn't it a hundred?"

I said, "Excuse me?"

He replied, "Why wasn't it a hundred?" Then he asked, "Did you try as hard as you could? Could you have tried a *little* harder?"

His question pierced my soul. He was challenging me to do my very best, not to settle for less than my best. He wasn't being cruel; in his own way, he was teaching me the leadership lessons I use today in my life and leadership program.

This C.H.A.I.R. Is for You

Whether I'm on stage giving a presentation or engaged in individual conversations, at some point my audience will ask about my leadership path in politics and business. Among my accomplishments, creating the C.H.A.I.R. Leadership program is one of the most satisfying because I'm on a mission to help others achieve their goals and realize their dreams by pulling up their "chair" and making their way toward success. In the chapters that follow, you will find insights, direction, and strategies that have made me successful … all of which you can apply to your life, and I am here to coach and encourage you on your journey.

As you delve into this book, you will discover the power behind the words in C.H.A.I.R. I challenge you to ponder each page individually and each chapter as a whole, then begin to figure out how to apply what you are reading to your personal and professional life.

This is not a one-and-done book. It isn't a book that you read and say, "That's great!" then move on to your next one. This is a book to read and *reread*. It is a book that will give you strategies to implement that can drastically and radically change your life … *if* you practice, practice, practice what you are about to read.

I've been doing exactly that—practicing, implementing, and mastering the strategies within these pages for over twenty-five years. Now, I want to coach you on your journey to do the same. A great thing about life is there's always something new to learn, a new way to challenge yourself, a new aha moment that comes along, and I want to help you master those moments.

> **You have to pick a path to follow and choose a direction to go in.**

There's a saying in business: you don't have to "boil the ocean." That means you can't take on everything and fail to accomplish anything. You have to pick a path to follow and choose a direction to go in. But which path? And what direction? This book will answer both of those questions for you. Within these pages, you will read about *five actionable strategies* with practical tips for application that will help you walk the path and take the direction that is right for you. As you understand, apply, and practice these time-tested strategies, using this book as your guide, you will empower yourself to set goals that you can truly achieve.

This book is a road map, a practical manual, a transformative guide to self-leadership and leading others. As you read, I'd like you to keep something in mind. Throughout my career, I have been the only woman in many boardrooms across the country, often the only person of color, and the only woman of color. I've also been the youngest person to serve in particular roles. I've led transformational initiatives and produced results that have been celebrated as milestone achievements. So if you feel you're an underdog, I've been in your shoes. If you have been successful but want to achieve even more, I'm in your corner.

> If you feel you're an underdog, I've been in your shoes.

As you apply what you learn, you will educate and empower yourself. You will learn and engage by challenging your own mindset and beliefs—about yourself and others. You will be able to shift your perspective, which can open new doors of opportunity and success. Feel free to dog-ear the pages, scribble notes in the margins, and add Post-it notes. Leadership is a lifelong journey—a marathon, not a sprint—and this book will affirm, equip, and empower you.

This C.H.A.I.R. Is about You

As you read through this book, remember this: C.H.A.I.R. is about you. It is about leading yourself *first*. I once heard someone say, "If you can't lead yourself, you can't lead others." That is so true. I firmly believe that my life illustrates this self-application, and I'm sure you can identify with the same at some level.

The first summer I was out of college, my father told me, "I want you to work on a factory assembly line." (My father had spent his working career doing just that.) He then added, "I want you to understand the value of hard work, to understand the value of the experiences that you're being afforded, and the education you're getting."

I tried hard to get out of it, but when my father said he wanted us to do something, that meant it really wasn't a choice. Here is the rub: The job was an hour and a half away from my house. I had to wake up every morning at 4:00 a.m. to get there by 6:00 a.m., work until 3:00 p.m., come home, and do it all over again the next day. I did this for an entire summer, and I was miserable. My mother was my saving grace that summer. She knew how dejected I was, so she woke me up every morning at 4:00 a.m. to ensure I left the house on time. What I learned from that experience far outweighed what I was paid—work ethic, commitment, keeping your word, doing the hard work. That experience stays with me to this day.

As a young woman, I had no idea how these lessons would benefit me in the long run. But one thing I did know: no one was going to live my life for me. As I look back, the self-discipline I developed that summer has stayed with me, and I've realized that self-discipline is a foundational building block to self-leadership.

Now let's focus on you. Before you read any further, here's your first assignment. Take a pen and a blank sheet of paper, or open up a Word document on your computer, and write down the following:

- What are your leadership goals?

- What makes you different from others?

- How does your answer to the previous question impact your leadership journey?

- Write down a word, phrase, or quote that motivates you.

You will need all these pieces of information as you continue to read.

Are you ready to take your seat at the table? Great!

Pull up a "chair" and get ready to learn and apply five actionable strategies that can drastically—and radically—take your self-leadership skills and ability to lead others to the next level!

All my best,

Cicely Simpson

WELCOME TO C.H.A.I.R. LEADERSHIP

Change begins at the end of your comfort zone.
—*ROY T. BENNETT*

To all of my readers, welcome to C.H.A.I.R. Leadership! I am sure you are excited, and I am just as excited for you. I know that you are ready to learn, to change, to grow, to become a better version of yourself. The fact that you have purchased this book tells me you are a leader, and you understand that you must lead yourself before you can lead others.

Before you go any further, I want to set the stage for everything that will come later.

You are about to discover five actionable strategies spelled out in the word "C.H.A.I.R." that you can apply to your life and when leading others. We are going to cover the strategies one by one, then discuss how to apply them to your situation. At the end of each chapter, I will give you practical tips and takeaways along with three to five action items, so that you can implement what you are learning.

Okay, let's get started.

What Is C.H.A.I.R. Leadership?

C.H.A.I.R. is a set of five actionable strategies that can radically and drastically change your leadership skills as you continue down your professional journey. C.H.A.I.R. is based on tried-and-true strategies that I have used to advance to the highest levels in my career. I have taught these strategies for years, and I am excited to share them with you. I am going to challenge you to be open to new behaviors as you navigate your leadership journey in ways you have not tried before.

C.H.A.I.R. stands for these qualities:

- Champion yourself

- Honesty

- Adaptability

- Impact

- Regrets

I have worked in government agencies, law firms, the US Congress, corporations, and trade associations. Being in these positions was a testament to hard work and perseverance. And those experiences are what C.H.A.I.R. Leadership is based on.

Why Is C.H.A.I.R. Important?

My goal is to meet you where you are, regardless of what stage of your career you are in. These strategies work regardless of age or position. I have coached students who are looking for their first job with these strategies. I have also coached CEOs who want to increase their influence with their teams and their boards of directors.

As you go through each chapter, you will read about my experiences that were trial and error. I will also coach you to "try this" or "say that" and see what happens. Remember: C.H.A.I.R. is about you—your self-leadership, your leadership of others, and gaining the successes in your career that you are looking for.

This stuff works *if* you implement and practice what you will learn.

Getting the Most out of This Book

As you read through these pages, I encourage you to *take your time*. This information is going to be new to you, so take time to understand and learn what you are reading. If you are the type of person who wants to read through the entire book and add your highlights first, then go back through and reread what you have noted, that's fine. If you prefer to work through each chapter, each section, and each page at a slower pace, that's fine too. Just make sure you absorb the information. An old choir director used to say, "Practice doesn't make perfect. Perfect practice makes perfect." But remember that perfection takes a lifetime.

Having the right attitude is so important. What is the right attitude? One that says, "I don't know everything; I'm open to new ideas and new ways of thinking."

It is important to read through the book, and take notes, in chronological order. Each chapter builds on the previous one, so don't skip over something just because you think you "already know that."

The C.H.A.I.R. model contains information you need to reach the goals you want to accomplish. There is no fluff here. The stories and illustrations will be pertinent to your leadership journey, giving you real-life, applicable, and actionable examples.

Here's the bottom line: your success is my success. This book is my investment in you, and I am here to support you. After you finish reading, I can continue to help you through my C.H.A.I.R. Leadership course (https://chair-leadership.teachable.com/), which also includes an exclusive Facebook community group. Or you can sign up for one-on-one coaching at www.cicelysimpson.com.

Your success is my success.

The Road Ahead

As you will see, each chapter includes a section called "The Road Ahead." It is one thing to have information presented to you; it's another thing to determine how to apply the information to your life going forward.

Application starts in your mind; it starts your thoughts and beliefs about yourself. Your mindset matters. If you live in your comfort zone, my goal is to change that mindset. Years ago, I had an executive coach who would challenge me to get comfortable with being uncomfortable. Being uncomfortable is where real growth and change occurs, and I am going to coach you in the same way my executive coach challenged me.

As noted in the preface, I want you to identify a word/phrase/quote that motivates you. Keep whatever you chose handy. You might want to write it on a sticky note and put it near your computer. You can create a banner or sign that you post around your living or office space. Whatever you do,

Your mindset matters.

your motivator should be kept in plain sight. Some days are harder than others, and you need that motivation to keep you going and pushing forward.

Do you remember the controversial Peloton commercial that was released where the guy was criticized for giving his wife the bike as a present? If you listen to the words in that commercial, the instructor says, "You didn't wake up to be mediocre today." While others saw criticism, I saw motivation. That phrase is on the home screen of my phone, and I repeat it often: "I didn't wake up to be mediocre. I didn't wake up to be mediocre." That is my motivation each and every day. Each day is a gift; what you do with it is entirely in your control.

"C"— CHAMPION YOURSELF

A note to my readers:

I am so excited that you are taking this journey toward self-leadership! By doing so, you are telling me that you're ready for more—more from yourself and more from your career.

By now, you have a solid understanding of my C.H.A.I.R. Leadership model, and you are ready to grow, to change, to become the leader you are meant to be in your career and your life.

As you continue reading, I want you to think about something: every building starts with a solid foundation. The foundation has to hold the entire weight of the building for decades, even centuries to come. As you well know, if the foundation starts to develop cracks, the entire building will be affected.

As you move through this book, I want you to be cognizant of the fact that you are starting with the letter "C"—champion yourself. I cannot stress enough how foundational it is for your career—and your success!—to fully understand what it means to champion yourself. So don't rush through this section. Be sure to make notes, highlight what stands out to you, and start to apply what you are learning as soon as possible.

Every building starts with a solid foundation.

Now repeat after me:

> What am I going to learn to do? Champion myself.
>
> What am I going to put into practice? How to champion myself.
>
> Why is championing myself so important? My career and success depend on it.

CHAPTER

RAISE YOUR HAND

BE YOUR BEST CHAMPION

Change your words, change your world.
—*CICELY SIMPSON*

What comes to mind when you think of the word "champion"? A sports team gathered around a trophy? An individual holding up a gold medal? Or someone standing on the top of a mountain yelling, "I did it!"

Consider there are champions in every sphere of life, including personal, career, politics, and sports. The word "champion" has two distinct definitions: first, a person who has defeated or surpassed all rivals in a competition; and second, a person who fights or argues for a cause, either personally or on behalf of someone else.

You might be thinking, *I've never conquered rivals or won competitions. I don't have a cause to fight for or advocate for someone else.* In reality, you have! Reading this book means you are someone who doesn't want to settle for second best. You want to push yourself further and deeper. You have mental toughness but want more. Congratulations! You have already conquered rivals who have said, "This is just too hard" and are not willing to change. The cause you are fighting for is you, and the person you are advocating for is yourself. In other words, to find your voice, you must be your own best champion.

The word "champion" is actionable and visual. A champion trains their thoughts to produce a total approach to performance. A champion understands their weaknesses and trains to strengthen them. That is you!

Notice that I am not using the word "confidence." The "C" does not stand for confidence. I chose "champion" for a reason.

"Confidence" is such a loaded word; you can have all the confidence in the world, but confidence alone will not get you what you want. For example, you could say, "I'm confident I can do the job." But you still have to go out and prove yourself.

That is why the word "champion" is such a powerful motivator.

Learning how to be your best champion can produce exponential results and is the single best thing you can do to advance yourself! When you champion yourself, you are being proactive instead of reactive or, even worse, passive. Remember this: don't use excuses … they are simply obstacles to your success. Excuses are an attempt to justify, defend, or blame-shift. Champions, however, take responsibility and ownership. They don't "sit and stink" in pity parties when something goes wrong or doesn't go their way. Instead, champions figure out what to do to make corrections and move forward.

I'm here to encourage and push you to champion yourself by looking at what you have, not what you don't have; looking at who you are, not at who you are not; looking at what you are capable of, not what you lack.

Keep this in mind: champions are not born; they are made. They are forged on the anvil of life.

When I speak to individuals and groups about leadership and professional development, "be your best champion" is the first principle I mention to every audience.

You are your best champion.

Let me say that again: you are your best champion.

Better yet, say it out loud: I am my best champion.

Championing yourself means it is your responsibility to own your growth and advancement, regardless of your role. Whether you are a CEO, someone just starting out in your career and the professional journey, or somewhere in between, you must advocate for yourself.

I repeat: to champion yourself is to advocate for yourself. It is the only way to succeed.

You might be thinking, *I've never thought of myself as a champion. Yes, I've conquered some territories in life, but I sure didn't have a clue what I was doing before I started. And when I look to the future, I can see areas that I'm not prepared to conquer.* That is okay; that is where all champions start.

Perhaps you are a person who already champions yourself as a self-advocate. That's great! As you continue to read, you will find affirmations in what you are doing, as well as additional strategies to use.

My Background

I have championed my skills, talents, and value at every stage in my career. In 1996, I received a bachelor of arts degree in political science from Lipscomb University. In 2001, I received a juris doctor degree from Pepperdine Caruso School of Law. I began my career in 1999 at the Tennessee Attorney General's Criminal Division before joining the law firm of Lewis, King, Krieg & Waldrop in Nashville in 2000, for my legal internship, then I went back to the firm in 2001 after graduation.

In 2002, I moved into politics as the legislative director for two Tennessee congressmen on Capitol Hill in Washington, US Rep. Lincoln Davis and US Rep. Jim Cooper in 2005. I then in 2008 moved on to become vice president of government affairs at Dunkin' Brands Inc., the franchisor and corporate parent of Dunkin' Donuts and Baskin-Robbins restaurants. During my tenure, I led the company's legislative, regulatory, and political strategy with federal, state, local, and international governments. A few years later, I became the executive vice president of public affairs at the National Restaurant Association, leading the restaurant industry's public affairs strategy at all levels of government to achieve the industry's public policy and political goals. In 2018, I founded and launched a lobbying and communications firm, Summit Public Affairs, and currently serve as the firm's CEO. I named the firm after the legendary women's basketball coach at the University of Tennessee, Pat Summitt. Coach Summitt was an amazing person and coach, someone I had the chance to work with and someone I deeply admire. She personified excellence and coached many champions throughout her life.

During my career, I have mastered the C.H.A.I.R. model, even though I may not have realized it at the time. Some of the positions I've held were not even created before I stepped into a particular government or corporate arena. I learned early to *champion* myself and say, "Hey, I have this and this to offer … you need me in your organization." I learned to be *honest* with myself—what I knew about a particular job position and what I needed to learn. I wasn't afraid to ask about things I didn't understand or to learn what I needed to know. I was quick to *adapt* to circumstances and situations that presented themselves. I may not have had the experience, but I remained open to mentoring from others, to learning whatever I needed to, and, most important, not limiting myself to my own thinking. I was determined to have an *impact* on whatever I was doing and whomever I was doing it for. And I wanted to live my life and have a career with no *regrets*.

I don't share any of this information to brag. The truth is I didn't have much of a clue as to what I was doing whenever I changed career paths. In some cases, I applied for positions that I was told I did not have the qualifications for. In others, I had to create a role from scratch. But in all situations, I was not afraid to create the conversation and say, "Here I am. This is what I can offer you."

For example, when I left law and moved into politics, I did not have any political experience. When I moved to Capitol Hill in 2002, I did not have legislative experience. When I transferred to the restaurant industry in 2008, working for Dunkin' Brands, I had no prior experience in the restaurant industry and was not quite sure what was involved in opening a government affairs office in Washington. But I knew what attributes I brought to the table, and I knew I could succeed if given the chance. I championed myself. Literally.

Case in point. My first interview was with an individual who was advising Dunkin' Brands on how to hire an in-house lobbyist in Washington. I knew very little about him; my only data point was that he knew the same of members of Congress I worked for. I'll spare you all of the details and simply say that when he and I met, I knocked it out of the park. We talked about the members we knew, but I also explained to him how my experience in Congress would benefit the company, and why the company should hire me. I talked about my success leading the legislative agenda for two congressmen, my success in building relationships with Democrats and Republicans in both the House and Senate, and my work ethic. In short, I convinced him the company needed me in this role. A week later, I flew to Key Biscayne, Florida, to interview with the chief communications officer while he was on vacation with his family. Then I got the job offer. All of this happened over the course of ten days. It was incredible!

Please hear me when I say I am no one special. I simply chose to raise my hand, open my mouth, and say, "I can do ..." I knew I could do the job if given the chance. I am no different from you, so no matter what arena you work in, you can do the same. But you have to decide to believe in yourself and champion yourself. Go ahead. Do that now. Decide right now that you will be your own best champion.

Champion yourself, and you will succeed.

A champion has a lifting effect; champions lift themselves to a higher plain and lift everyone around them. Everybody has a champion or knows what their idea of a champion is—someone who is at the top of their game or craft and has reached the highest levels of success they are seeking. There is immediate visual association with that word that makes it actionable and impactful, positive, and empowering.

Always remember this: champion yourself, and you will succeed.

Why Champion Yourself?

I recently coached a client who said, "I don't want to raise my hand in meetings because I don't have anything to offer."

If you read between the lines, this client wanted to disqualify herself due to her lack of confidence in who she is and what she has to offer. I had to challenge my client: "You really don't have *anything* to offer?" She paused for a few moments, then went on to list several things to potentially contribute. I watched my client's face light up and her body language change—she believed in herself!

When you champion yourself, you must be aware of times that you automatically disqualify yourself. Then you must challenge yourself to figure out why you do that. What is your reason or motive? Do you even realize what you are doing?

Whether in my public affairs business or coaching a client, I often hear the reluctance, the apprehension, the uncomfortableness that some people have with proactively championing their success and growth. The sad truth is that some people just *expect* others to notice who they are and what they are doing. I hear, "If I do a good job, my boss will notice," and "If I do a good job, my peers will recognize it."

No, they won't.

Or if they do, rarely will you be acknowledged.

I'll cover this in more detail in the next chapter, but let's face it, your boss and your peers are all busy. Don't assume others see the value you add every day. Don't assume they understand all the contributions you make to the team and organization. Don't assume they know your accomplishments and successes.

I know that sounds harsh, but you have to be realistic. You must reorient your thinking toward letting others know your value, contributions, and accomplishments—and that is where being your own best champion starts.

Your leadership journey is about you. It is about your trajectory, your success, and where you want to go. You have to be willing to take those chances to raise your hand, to speak up, and to speak out. Certainly, you are risking that you might not be received, or maybe you are taking a chance on failing, but there are ways to minimize that risk.

I talked about Shirley Chisholm earlier, and she is truly one of my heroes. She was the first female African American elected to Congress (1968) and the first woman and African American to seek the nomination for president of the United States from one of the two major political parties (1972). The former vice chair of the House Democratic Caucus, her motto and title of her autobiography—*Unbossed and Unbought*—illustrates her outspoken advocacy for women and minorities during her seven terms in the US House of Representatives.[1] I encourage you to always remember her famous quote: "If they don't give you a seat at the table, bring a folding chair."

From this point forward, I want you to visualize yourself carrying a folding chair wherever you go. You might be in a meeting at work or on a Zoom call. You might be with your family at home. Perhaps you are at a gathering with friends. Are there times when you fail to say something, even though everything within you says to speak up?

---

1   Debra Michaels, "Shirley Chisholm," National Women's History Museum, 2015,
      https://www.womenshistory.org/education-resources/biographies/shirley-chisholm.

Are there times you want to say, "Hey, I'm here!" but you don't? If so, start to ask yourself, "Why don't I?" Then, when you have your answer, ask yourself, "What do I want to do about it?"

I want to be clear about something. Championing yourself does not mean pushing your way through and having a get-out-of-my-way attitude. It is about stating what your credentials are, why you are the right person for whatever you are going after, and how you can help contribute to the overall success. You want to be the person who pulls up a chair to the table, the one who raises their hand. It is about who you are, what you have to offer, and why you are the right person.

This Is About You

During a recent virtual "Dream. Believe. Create." career and business summit, I talked about the five strategies of C.H.A.I.R. Leadership:

- Champion yourself
- Honesty
- Adaptability
- Impact
- Regrets

The host of the summit later noted these strategies had a profound impact on him. He was facing a tough situation: he was doubted and questioned his capabilities and qualifications.

He knew he had a choice, the same choice all of us have in any situation when faced with *fear*: face everything and run *or* face everything and rise.

To champion yourself, you must show up differently. You have to do what is necessary to overcome your fears and find your voice. You have to rise to meet the moment, be ready to explain your value, your expertise, and that, in fact, you are more than good enough—you are ready to take on the challenge. You must also be willing to walk away rather than compromise your value.

The summit host was willing to meet his challenge … and he was willing to walk away, if necessary.

Have you been in a similar situation? Where your value has been questioned? When you were told your experience was not good enough? When someone caused you to doubt yourself? Are you disappointed because your second-guessing caused you to miss an opportunity?

You are not alone.

All of us have been there. The hardest part is the feeling of doubt and disappointment in yourself.

It's okay to have those moments of disappointment. The key is to make sure they are *only moments and not a permanent mindset*. Don't forget there is a lot of you inside. Take some time to reassess your amazing qualities. Even though there are hard days, you can and will find your inner strength again. As your coach, I'm here to tell you that you will get through your moments of doubt with your strength intact because of how strong you truly are.

Countless people have been in similar situations. What separates those who move forward, who get ahead, from those who settle for average and lose out comes down to whether or not someone is willing to champion themselves.

Ask yourself, "Do I know my value and the contributions I have to offer?"

Keep in mind that today's no can be tomorrow's yes—*if* you determine that you will not be deterred from your goal. Do not let other people project their insecurities onto you. It is good to listen to different viewpoints, but you have to make decisions that are the best for you. You cannot live your life for someone else, according to someone else's views and opinions.

Stay positive. Be willing to talk about your contributions, your value, your accomplishments, and why you should raise your hand and let people know about what you have to offer.

Let's get specific. Let's say you have your annual review coming up within the month. Have you thought about what you are going to say?

First of all, take a timeout. Your review should be viewed as an opportunity, not a challenge. How do you make it an opportunity?

Three words:

1. Value

2. Contributions

3. Accomplishments

That's it. Seriously, that's it. Allow me to explain.

Your reviews, conversations about promotions, salary increases, whatever the conversation may include, should be viewed as an opportunity to champion yourself:

- Remind your manager and the organization about the value you add and why you are an asset to the organization.

- Discuss what you have contributed toward team goals and organizational goals.

- Celebrate and list your accomplishments—how your contributions and value ensured your success and the organization's progress and success.

Don't make it complicated. This is about you and only you. You are not trying to "people please"; you want your manager to see you in the best light. Keep in mind they may know what you do but may not be aware of the details. For example, you may have gone the extra mile on several projects to help others or to bring about a successful conclusion. But if you wait until the last minute to remember these details, it is easy for your mind to feel stressed, and you forget what you have accomplished. Here is a pro tip: track this information on your calendar or in a spreadsheet, and use it whenever your reviews come up to advocate for yourself. When it is time for the meeting, have a bulleted list ready to share with your manager. Think of this information as the "*you*" list. Start your "*you*" list now—it is one of the most valuable tools I offer in this book, and it works!

The "*you*" list is your road map to championing yourself. This map includes the following:

- Your value: What skills and experience do you bring to the table?

- Your contributions: What are you currently doing?

- Your accomplishments: What successes can you present?

- Your lessons: What have you learned that will be a benefit?

As you continue to read the rest of the book, you'll be able to put your own "*you*" list together.

I recently had a coaching client who is an amazingly talented person. However, everything she does is through the lens of her job and company strategies. I said to her, "We've been talking for some time now about all the processes and procedures you follow and your role in the company, but where are *you* in all of this?"

She looked at me wide eyed for a few moments. Then she started thinking. Finally, she said, "I've never talked about what I can do, how I can add value, and how I can lead."

I began to challenge her to bring herself into conversations. That did not mean every sentence had to be about her, but I wanted her to make sure she was articulating clearly about what she had done, and what she had to offer. I wanted her to see how she was managing herself and promoting her strengths, and how they played into what the company was looking for. Then I challenged her to create her "*you*" list.

A couple of weeks later, her big moment came. There was a leadership role she had wanted for some time, and she scheduled an appointment with her manager to talk about what she needed for this role. Beforehand, we talked about two things. First, to have her "*you*" list ready so she could competently advocate as to why she should get promoted to a leadership role. Second, I coached her to understand that even if she didn't get this role during the conversation with her manager, she must not let the conversation end unless her manager commits to helping her develop a leadership plan, a road map to get her to the next level.

Do you see my point? She advocated for herself in two ways: first, communicating the value she could add in this new leadership role; and second, securing the commitment to develop a leadership plan for her, if this role was not the right fit.

At this point, I'm sure you are wondering, *What happened? Did she get the promotion?* She got the promotion!

My client is a great example of how to champion yourself, and I encourage you to do the same. If you don't keep track of your contributions, your accomplishments, and the value you bring to the table (the "*you*" list), who will?

If you don't state clearly why you deserve the role you are going after, don't expect someone else to be your champion. I am not saying that someone else will not do this for you, but I am saying don't *expect* someone to step forward on your behalf. You have to raise your hand. You have to let people know you have the confidence to do the job.

Remember, when you start to implement the strategies you are learning, don't think you are going to conquer the world the first time. Once you have your "*you*" list of your value, contributions, and accomplishments, distill this list down to the most important points you want to convey. You do not need pages and pages of notes. Keep this simple through bullet points and short lists. Start small to set yourself up for success. Success breeds success! Internalize what you need to say, how you need to say it, and to whom you need to say it. You will be amazed at how you set yourself up with confidence, so you can speak clearly and articulate your message, knowing that it is well received. Practice exactly how you are going to advocate for yourself. Rehearse situations and conversations that you might face, so you are ready when the time comes.

Advocating for yourself is not a once-or-twice-a-year exercise. You need to bring your A game and be your best champion every single day.

R-E-S-P-E-C-T Yourself

If you want to excel at championing yourself, it is imperative that you have respect for yourself ... all day, every day. Self-respect means that you have pride and confidence in yourself; you feel and behave with honor and dignity toward yourself. Being your best champion starts with self-respect. You need to know and acknowledge to yourself that you have value, worth, and potential. It starts with you. If you do not have confidence in your abilities, who will? Self-respect will banish thoughts of self-doubt. You are your best—and sometimes only— advocate with the power to enact change in your life, and at times in the lives of others. Give yourself permission to support yourself in the same way you would support others.

Respecting starts by defining your own worth and value as a person. You have to be clear in your own mind about who you are and your importance to yourself. So take a look in the mirror—a good hard look—and ask yourself, "Am I more critical of myself or confident in myself? Do I see the good and the value I bring to others, to a project, and to my work?" Think about this: If you do not respect yourself, how can you expect others to respect you? It all begins with self-respect.

I do the very thing I'm asking you to do—I respect and support myself every single day, even though there may be certain situations I am not completely sure of, or confident in, what I am doing. I don't focus on the unknown; I focus on my abilities that will get me through the unknown.

Steps to Champion Yourself

While working in my law career, I moved back to Nashville and reconnected with a friend with whom I went to college. We got together one night, and he told me he was working for a state senator who was running for Congress, and they needed someone who could do some policy advising and help with talking points. He added, "It would be good for you to get reconnected back to the Tennessee political scene."

"Sure, it would be fun to work during the day at the law firm and help you out at night," I replied, wondering how I would juggle all the work.

Toward the end of the campaign, I transitioned to a role helping the campaign full time, even though I was not sure the senator would win. But I felt it was the right move at that point in my career. When election night came in 2002, to everyone's pleasant surprise, the senator won the congressional seat. During the celebration, he said to me, "Cicely, how do you feel about going to Washington?"

I stared at him for a few moments, then said, "You know I'm from a small rural town. Why would I ever go to Washington?"

He smiled and said, "Well, come be part of our team."

As we talked, he mentioned the legislative director position, and he felt that I would be a good fit. Legislative director? I did not even know what that meant!

When I talked to my parents, they thought it was the craziest thing they had heard of—me, going to Washington. But the day after Christmas, 2002, I moved to Capitol Hill to lead a freshman member of Congress and his congressional staff and to help him set up his office.

I can tell you that if there is anywhere you have to be your best champion, it is Washington. I had to learn to speak up—fast. I had to raise my hand often. I had to advocate all the time ... for myself and for the congressman.

In that role as his legislative director, I learned quickly that being your own best champion starts with your mindset. And I had to quickly learn how to change my mindset to embracing new possibilities. Always remember, being your own best champion starts with your mindset.

The trouble with mindsets is that we too often see the negative instead of the positive. Here are some ways you can have a champion's mindset:

1. *Think of past experiences where you have succeeded.* It might have been in business, on your career path, or something personal like making a sports team or getting a first date with

someone you have been wanting to ask out. Picture the event and feel the feelings you had. Then transfer this imagery to whatever you are contemplating doing in the present. Always remember, practice, practice, practice right before you need to perform, and you will be amazed at your confidence level.

2. *Motivate yourself.* Championing yourself means you are not looking for someone or something else to motivate you; it comes from within. One of the best ways to self-motivate is to constantly be thinking about your "why": Why am I doing this? Why do I want to do that? Motivation will spur you through the low times and will reinforce what you are doing in the good times.

3. *Know that nothing is impossible.* When it comes to the unknown, it is normal to doubt. But when you champion yourself, you don't stay in the negative. Instead, you look for ways to move forward, to overcome the obstacle, to get around the roadblock.

4. *Always give 100 percent.* Every day is a new day! It is a chance to start over, to move on, or to build on what you accomplished yesterday. Giving 100 percent means giving your best and performing at your highest level. Remember my personal motto I shared earlier? "I didn't wake up to be mediocre." Feel free to adopt the same mindset.

5. *Take responsibility.* This is a big one. When things go south, it is easy to deflect responsibility and to point fingers. When that happens, be willing to take responsibility where needed and move on. Don't get caught up in blaming, gossip, or anything negative. Your goal is to learn from mistakes—your own and others'—and to constantly improve, to set new

goals and challenges. Doing so will make you stronger and keep you focused on future success.

As you close this chapter, I want to congratulate you! You've done some hard work by taking a good look at yourself and what you need to do to champion yourself. This isn't easy; what *is* easy is maintaining the status quo. But the status quo won't get you to where you want to go. As you continue to read, I challenge you to continue with a can-do mindset.

Pull Up Your C.H.A.I.R.— Action Items

As your coach, I encourage you to take these actions:

- Raise your hand and be willing to advocate for yourself, to say, "I believe that I am qualified for X because of Y." Or "Based on my experience in X and the results I have achieved, I am a good fit for this role."

- Talk about your role on a team—not just on a high level but your specific contributions.

- Raise your hand for an opportunity or to lead a project or a cross-functional assignment that may come up.

- Don't sit there and wait to be assigned something. Proactively engage to seek the outcome that you want.

CHAPTER

2

HOPE IS NOT
A STRATEGY

HOW TO CHAMPION YOURSELF

If you have an idea, you have to believe in yourself, or no one else will.
—SARAH MICHELLE GELLAR

We all need hope. Without it, we would lose inspiration and motivation to do whatever it is we want to accomplish. Hope is like gasoline to a car engine; it is the fuel the engine needs to start and keep the car moving forward.

You may not have heard of Hal Elord, but he is a man who never lost hope.

Early in his life, Hal was like most of society—a regular person with regular aspirations. I would call him a middle-of-the-road type of person. But one day, life changed for Hal forever.

Hal clinically "died" at age twenty. He was hit head on by a drunk driver at seventy miles per hour, and his heart stopped for six minutes.

Hope, by itself, is *not* a strategy.

When he eventually woke from a coma, he found out that he had eleven broken bones and was told by doctors that he would never walk again. However, not only did Hal walk, he went on to run an ultramarathon (fifty-two miles!) and become a hall of fame business achiever—before the age of thirty. He also wrote a life-changing book titled *The Miracle Morning*.

While Hal might have lost a lot of things during his ordeal, there is one thing he never lost: hope.

Hope is inspiration. It is the excitement behind the "What ifs?" It is the fuel that drives the engine of creativity. Hope allows us to dream—big! When there are no limitations, our minds soar with hope beyond the clouds, the sky, and into the heavens above. When you have hope powering your dream, and you're determined to do the necessary work, then you are ready to champion yourself.

However, hope, by itself, is *not* a strategy. What I mean is you cannot lay out a plan of action based on hope. And in a professional context, hope can give you a false sense of security.

I have been on both sides of the "hope" conversation. I have been in an employee role, and I have been in a leadership/manager role. As an employee, you hope people notice the great job you are doing. You hope your boss and peers recognize the great job you are doing and how much of an asset you are to the team.

But what if they don't notice?

The worst feeling is to expect compliments, accolades, and promotions, but they never happen.

In the leadership/manager role, I cannot tell you how many times my team members would come to me and ask me why they didn't receive a promotion, why they were not appointed to a special project, or why they did not get the compliments they thought would come their way. I cannot tell you how many times I've heard, "I thought you knew."

My response was always the same: "Why didn't you ask for a conversation with me? Why are these accomplishments not on your self-assessment? Why didn't you bring them up in your review?"

They *hoped* I knew the work they did every day. They *hoped* I noticed the great job they did on that cross-functional team or how they handled a certain situation.

As I think back, I have kicked myself on more occasions than I want to admit for making the same mistakes. Too many times, I had hoped that someone knew something about me or what I had accomplished, and I've learned the hard way—if I don't say it, they may not know, and if I don't say it, they may never know.

What I'm telling you is that hope by itself is not a strategy. That may sound harsh, but please hear me when I say that hope does not put feet to the path or pen to paper, nor does it do the necessary work. I'll say it again: hope is not a strategy. As your coach, I want to help you reorient your thinking toward nothing but success. With hope as your fuel, you won't see anything but success as your only option, and you will not settle for anything less than what you want to achieve. But you still need to turn hope into action. If you want people to notice you, then you have to stand up and be noticed. There is no other option, and you shouldn't settle for anything less than what you want to achieve. Period. Be realistic about any limitations, but do not simply accept that seemingly impossible obstacles cannot be overcome. Instead, look over, around, or past any encumbrances. Don't simply "hope" these will go away—that will never happen.

The good news is that if others know how valuable you are and what great work you do, then championing yourself demonstrates that you are a strong leader capable of the growth you seek. It is your responsibility to make sure your boss and peers know the value you are adding every day. It is your responsibility to champion yourself. If you don't do it, no one will do it for you.

You will notice the subtitle of this chapter is "how" to champion yourself. The word "how" entails taking action. Those who champion themselves don't hear something inspiring and say, "Oh, that's nice," then go on about their business. Instead, when something resonates within them, they take action, such as talking out an idea with a trusted person, creating plans to achieve, or whatever else is needed.

The "how" means you are purposeful and intentional about your growth, your success, and your dreams.

The word "purpose" means the reason for which something is done or created or for which something exists. The word "intentional" necessitates that you make decisions and take actions that align with your priorities. Being purposeful and intentional requires getting clear in your mind what you want to achieve and bringing your outcome into reality.

When you are purposeful and intentional, you are no longer hoping for a result. You are setting the stage for the results you want.

Now ask yourself, "How can I champion myself by being purposeful and intentional in ways that I am willing to stand up for?"

Advocating for Yourself

No matter what role I have held within an organization, I have created an ongoing list of my accomplishments, how I've added value to my team and the organization, the contributions I made to my team and the organization, and the lessons I've learned. In other words, I have always created my own "*you*" list that I referred to in chapter 1. I encourage you to keep this same list in regard to any situation you find yourself in. Remember, you are not trying to boil the ocean.

This list is very tactile, but also very strategic, and includes four items:

- Your value: What skills and experience do you bring to the table?

- Your contributions: What are you currently doing?

- Your accomplishments: What successes can you present?

- Your lessons: What have you learned that will be a benefit?

Once you have your list, you are ready for the opportunities to advocate for yourself, opportunities that manifest themselves in ways such as quarterly or yearly reviews, weekly meetings with your boss, monthly team meetings, cross-functional teams you are a part of ... the list is unending. The point is you will use the four items in your "*you*" list to advocate for yourself. Nothing more, nothing less. Just four items can make all the difference.

When you advocate for yourself, you are standing up for yourself. You are being your own voice. You are recognizing your contributions and letting others know as well.

When I first worked at Dunkin' Donuts, I had no idea what I was getting myself into. My role was new, the government affairs function was new, and no one knew why I was hired. To make matters worse, during my first week on the job, I had to meet with each executive leadership team member to tell them about my role and how I could help their team.

Talk about trial by fire!

But that was not the end.

I constantly had to answer the questions, "What do you do, and why are you here?" from random people for several months. Daily, I had to explain who I was and what value I brought. This was truly a crash course in advocating for myself.

I started my job in April 2008, but in the spring of 2009, my C-suite-level boss was fired by the new CEO. In fact, most of the executive team was fired and replaced. Soon after, I received a call from the new CEO telling me that my boss had been fired and to keep doing my job until given further instructions. I spent the next several months wondering if I would have a job, but I kept my head down and stayed focused on the tasks at hand.

In the fall of 2009, the CEO said he was coming to Washington and wanted to meet with me. On a crisp, clear autumn morning, we met for breakfast, which started out with a cordial tell-me-about-yourself conversation. But the small talk didn't last long. After taking a sip of coffee, he said, "We don't know what to do with you or your role. We can't decide whether to keep government affairs, have you report to legal, or have you report to communications or to someone else." Then he looked me square in the eye and said, "What should we do?"

I literally thought I was going to be fired!

As I drew in a breath, I quickly recalled the times I had to articulate what I do and how I bring value to the company. (Keep in mind this was right in the middle of the US economy's worst financial crisis in recent memory.) I then calmly explained to him my bipartisan relationships, how the financial crisis was impacting the company and our franchises, and why the company needed me.

His next statement was, "You haven't talked about healthcare. I'm interested in the healthcare system and why this country doesn't provide health insurance for all Americans."

I wish I had a recording of this conversation, because the look on my face must have been sheer panic.

Healthcare? Wait, what?

The Affordable Care Act was being debated in Congress, so clearly it was top of mind for my new CEO. I had to quickly formulate a way to explain this complex legislation to him in sound bites. I explained the goals of the bill, how I was working on the bill on Capitol Hill to help our franchisees, and how I thought we could have a greater impact on the debate and the outcome.

Oh, but it didn't stop there.

He said, "It is my understanding that you and our general counsel don't see eye to eye on whether federal or state legislation is the priority for our company." Then he eyed me again and asked, "Who is right … you or him?"

I kept my calm and answered respectfully why I disagreed with the GC, and why I thought my position was correct.

A few minutes later he said, "Okay. Nice to meet you."

With that, he paid the bill and left with a cordial goodbye.

Thankfully, that breakfast conversation saved my job, and working for that company was one of the best professional decisions I've made—all because I advocated for myself.

Let's switch back to you.

Take some time to think about when you have—and haven't—advocated for yourself. What were the outcomes? What did you learn? Now ask yourself, "Do I have the self-confidence to advocate for myself in my current or future roles?" If you feel a little shaky thinking about doing this, take a cue from my coaching playbook and write down on a daily, weekly, or monthly basis the value you bring to your company, the value you bring to your team, and what that value looks like: project initiatives, team meetings, research, etc. When the time comes to speak up for yourself, you'll feel confident and prepared.

Earlier, I said that hope, by itself, is not a strategy. "Hoping" for something is not preparation. "Hoping" will not get a promotion. Advocating for yourself, however, will move you down the path you want to take.

Think about the times you have advocated for yourself. I'm sure you will see that whenever you stepped up on your own behalf, you always felt better. And the times when you didn't, more than likely there are feelings of regret.

Staying on Track

One of the practical ways I have learned how to champion myself is by keeping my life on a schedule. I'm sure you have heard the saying, "What gets scheduled gets done." I live by that philosophy. If a meeting or phone call or time to work on a project is not on my calendar, then it is not getting done. I'm a big believer in setting aside time to do the work, setting aside time to relax, and so on. While how much time to spend on something varies for everyone, the fact is that keeping your life on a schedule means you are always in control. And believe it or not, being in control of your schedule allows for flexibility.

For instance, when you are in control of your time, you can determine if something needs to change, and you can allow for those inevitable emergencies that come up.

Keeping a schedule of what your day/week/month looks like allows you to achieve your goals and priorities in the time you have available. Why? Because a schedule forces you to stay focused on the task at hand while being aware of what is coming up. This helps you to

- understand what you can realistically accomplish within a set timeframe,

- give adequate time for priorities,

- allow time for the unexpected,

- avoid taking on more tasks or responsibility than you can handle,

- plan for and work steadily toward your goals, and

- achieve a healthy work-life balance.

Time is the one resource that we can't buy, but we often waste it or use it ineffectively. Scheduling helps you think about what you want to achieve in a day, week, or month, and it keeps you on track to accomplish your goals.

Practical Steps

Before you read this section, I want you to ponder this quote for a few moments:

If you really want to do something, you'll find a way.
If you don't, you'll find an excuse.
—JIM ROHN

Understanding that "hope is not a strategy" starts with knowing that you have to take action. Others do not know what you hope for; they only know what you do and what you say. Taking action each day moves you out of a I-hope-this-happens mindset and into a I'm-going-to-make-this-happen mindset.

Now, you might be saying, "But, Cicely, I don't know what I really want to do."

I hear you.

Ask yourself, "What truly inspires me? What do I love so much that I could do it twenty-four seven and not get tired of doing it, even when the inevitable challenges come?" Remember that inspiration drives purpose, and when inspiration and purpose align, you will find a way to make your dream a reality.

The core of the "hope is not a strategy" approach is that actions speak louder than words. Planning, preparation, and performance are more valuable actions than the ideas that only you know about. A strategy based on words and ideas without corresponding action is not going to succeed.

Striving to accomplish big dreams and bold goals can be scary and daunting. Sometimes, it's easy to make excuses for not getting what you really want. It's easy to give up. It's easy to acquiesce and say, "I guess it was never meant to be." Really? Those who know how to champion themselves find out what they need to do to get what they want … then they follow that path. So it is up to you to make sure you are proactively managing, proactively seeking success, finding a way to yes, and not taking no for an answer.

When the role at Dunkin' was first mentioned to me, I remember thinking, *Wow, it's a huge goal to establish a Washington office and business presence for a company that has never engaged in public policy before.* Remember, when I started at Dunkin', I had neither restaurant industry experience nor business experience. But I knew I wanted to work for this company. I wanted to be the person who could accomplish these big goals and successfully lead this company in Washington. When I started, I took pages and pages of notes from meetings, from research, and from what others were telling me, then I would go home and study them because I wanted to know the restaurant industry inside out. I wanted to become proficient and efficient, so that I could excel in this role.

You might be asking, "How does this relate to championing yourself?" When you champion yourself, you are pursuing whatever you put your mind to with dogged determination. It means you are *always* doing your best work. *You* are doing the work. It is amazing how you can step into your future when others know who you are and what you are doing. Your work and your reputation will precede you, and others will say, "We've got a new job (project, role, etc.), and I know the perfect person for this job."

Considering future possibilities, while staying focused in the present, is a unique skill that you can cultivate.

Between 2009 and 2010, my responsibilities at Dunkin' Donuts grew to include two additional streams of work. Initially, I was hired to work with the federal government, but as the need became evident, I was asked to add state governments and local governments to my job responsibilities. I was doing the work of a vice president, but my title and pay were at director level.

I had a decision to make: keep working and *hope* I get a promotion, or *ask* for the promotion.

I chose to make my case and ask for a promotion.

During my annual review, I was told all the reasons why I didn't meet the criteria to be a vice president. I could have easily succumbed to a defeatist mentality, thinking that my hopes had been dashed. But

I'll say it again: hope is not a strategy. Instead, I said to myself, "I am not taking no for an answer." Instead, I explained the work I was doing and asked to see the list of criteria I needed to meet for the promotion.

I asked my boss to create an action plan regarding what I needed to do to get to the vice president level. So we talked through each of the HR criteria I needed to meet. For instance, I needed to manage people but did not have a team. I then asked, "How do I get the resources to build a team? Can I rework my budget to make room for head count? What else do I need to do?"

My boss was great! We worked together to develop an eighteen-month plan of the work I needed to do with business units across the company to demonstrate the value I could offer to their teams and their work. That plan also involved work I needed to do to develop my leadership style. Our CEO signed off on the plan as well. I completed every one of the items in that plan, which enhanced my role and my understanding of the company tremendously. "How?" you might ask. I "gathered up the fragments of time" during my workday and in the evenings. I would take a few minutes here, an hour there, and a half day, when possible, to work on the points laid out in my plan.

Guess what? I met all the benchmarks and exceeded the expectations *before* the eighteen-month deadline! Do you want to know the best part? The company recognized my efforts with an award at a company leadership conference, *and* I received the promotion. That award, a crystal coffee cup inscribed with a message to me, sits in my office to this day.

I could have just hoped for the best and waited for someone to notice the great job I was doing, but instead I did the work necessary to achieve my goals.

Attitude Is Everything

In his book *Attitude Is Everything*, author Jeff Keller makes some great points about why our attitude determines our outlook and our future. He argues that, even in the worst-case scenarios, we have the option to choose our attitude and how we respond to a problem.

In understanding how to champion yourself, having the right attitude means deciding that your growth, your impact, and your success are worth your time and effort. This starts with being clear about your value and contributions, your strengths and accomplishments. It means being intentional, being purposeful.

When you think about the word "attitude," what comes to mind? Someone being snarky and mean? Someone who has a can-do mindset? Here is a word you might not think of: "doubt."

Doubt can change your attitude from positive to negative in a heartbeat. It can drag you down from the mountaintop to the lowest valley. But if you think about it, as long as you don't doubt yourself, then it does not matter what other people say; the only person you need to listen to is … you. Please, hear me out on this: you can do this. I know, because I learned to do this in a very practical way.

When I worked on Capitol Hill in 2005 for the Tennessee congressman, we were having a conversation one day, and I called him "Congressman."

He said, "Call me Jim."

I said, "No, Congressman."

He said, "Call me Jim."

I replied, "Look, I am not going to call you Jim. You have earned the title of Congressman, so I am going to call you Congressman."

He looked at me as seriously as he could and said, "Cicely, when you view yourself as an equal, you will be treated as an equal. You put your pants on one leg at a time, like everyone else."

Those two simple statements have stayed with me to this day. Anytime I doubt myself, I remind myself that if I view myself as an equal, I will be treated like an equal. I used to walk into the room and sit in the back. I didn't think it mattered where I sat. Not anymore. Equals sit at the table with other equals. As your coach, I encourage you to adopt that statement as your personal mantra, and repeat it anytime you feel doubt, anxiety, or worry.

Sure, you are going to be nervous at times. And you may find that very uncomfortable. You may be worried what others will think.

> **If I view myself as an equal, I will be treated like an equal.**

But when you are faced with a new opportunity, a new job, or a potential promotion, ask yourself, "Why not me?" Those three words will go a long way to quelling your doubts and boosting your attitude.

Think of your attitude in terms of this equation: energy = motion. Your attitude produces the energy you need to create motion. "Why not me?" is an attitude you need in order to move in a positive direction.

If you are doing the work, if you are exceeding expectations, then why not you? Don't let self-doubt defeat you. Ask yourself, "What is the worst that can happen?" You don't get what you are advocating for … right now. But if that happens, don't let the answer derail you. Remember, today's no is tomorrow's yes. Shrug it off and move on. Other opportunities will come along. When you finally get that yes, you will feel so much better knowing that you overcame the obstacles that were in your way because you maintained a can-do attitude.

As your coach, I want you to commit to

- advocating for a path that will get the promotion or new role you want;

- advocating for the raise you want and deserve;

- advocating to be part of the new initiative that was just launched;

- advocating to be a new manager or a new team leader; and

- advocating for a role for which you have no experience, but know that you can grow into the role and learn it.

In 2015, I left Dunkin' Donuts to become the executive vice president of public affairs for the restaurant industry. I had no idea how to be an EVP. I didn't know what the position entailed, nor did I have any training. But I had the right attitude, and I knew I was ready for the next level in my career. I wanted a role with a national profile and national platform to continue to build my brand.

During my interviews, I maintained a positive mindset and a self-advocate attitude, and I did not rely on "hope" as part of my strategy to get this position. I talked about why I could be an asset to the industry, my accomplishments in my previous role, and how I thought the industry could increase its impact at all levels of government. I explained my ideas, why I would be an asset to the industry, and why I was perfect for this role.

And that is how I got the job … after I turned it down multiple times. But that's another story.

Pull Up Your C.H.A.I.R.— Action Items

As your coach, I encourage you to take these actions:

- Start your "*you*" list: your value, contributions, accomplishments, and lessons learned.

- Ask yourself, "What can I do to grow in my current role, or what do I need to do to get the promotion I want or to move into a new role?"

- Get clarity on your passion and purpose.

- Is there an area that you need to advocate for yourself? If so, write out several ways you can "defeat your doubt."

- Reclaim the "fragments of time" that you can put to better use.

CHAPTER

3

TRACK YOUR BIG WINS AND SMALL TRIUMPHS

THE ROAD AHEAD

People don't decide their future, they decide their
habits, and their habits decide their future.
—*F. M. ALEXANDER*

I have been working with a smart, confident coaching client who has been working for her company for several years. She knows her job and does it well. The company always lets her know how valuable she is and how much she is appreciated. So what's the problem?

My client stated that is exactly the problem—she is valuable but not valued. She is appreciated but was always passed over for promotions. She is considered the tried-and-true go-to person by everyone, but she was not getting the leadership opportunities she wanted … and she was frustrated.

While working together, I unpacked her situation a little more by asking, "How do you show up? You say you are being recognized, but how are you championing yourself and advocating for yourself? How do you show up in meetings to get that feedback?"

At this point, she felt unsure. She knew she was a good team player. At the same time, whenever she was in a meeting, she wondered if they were having a tactical conversation or strategic conversation. She did not know when to speak up. After a meeting, she always followed up with an email to get clarity.

"Well, that's great," I replied. "Obviously you're comfortable with the feedback loop if you're following up. I encourage you to start showing up differently in your conversations with your boss and in meetings. When they say, 'Hey, you're a great member of the team,' that's great. But the question to ask is 'If I'm a great member of the team, why am I still in the same role getting passed over for jobs and promotions?'"

Over the course of several coaching sessions, I helped her to understand how to track her value, her contributions, and her accomplishments in detail every day, then how to distill them down so she had clarity on a few succinct details. This is her *"you"* list that she created, so that she is prepared to advocate for herself when the opportunity arises.

Just recently, the right time came for a conversation with her boss. And she was ready.

When he said, "You're one of the most valuable people in the organization," she asked him what, exactly, he meant by that. After he clarified, she asked, "What is the next step for me?" At that point, she knew she had two choices: ask for the leadership role she wanted and present her memorized list of qualifications and reasons she should have the job, or continue being a reserved team player.

She chose the former and advocated for the leadership role.

We had worked on language cues for how to say particular things. I also reminded her that if she didn't get the position, to consider using the strategy I mentioned in the last chapter: do not let the conversation end until he had helped her develop the road map to the next role. Was it a six- to twelve-month path? Twelve to eighteen? Either way, she knew she needed to come to the conversation with one of those two pieces.

I encouraged her to seize the moment to champion her growth, value, and contributions to the team and organization. If she was such a valuable member of the team, she needed to find out just how valuable, and what that value was going to translate to.

You know what? In that same conversation with her boss, she put herself first and decided not to settle for anything less than the role she wanted. I am thrilled to tell you that she got the leadership role! And I continue to support and cheer her success as she moves into the new position.

Smart Small

I've shared a lot of information with you in these first couple of chapters. If it feels like you are drinking from a fire hose of information, step back and take a deep breath. As the old saying goes, Rome wasn't built in a day, and you aren't going to conquer championing yourself in a day either. I realize I have given you a "go big or go home" type of strategy, but I encourage you to start small. Start where you are. The idea in creating your "*you*" list is not to try to capture everything you have done in your career. I encourage you to start where you are right now. Start tracking your wins, contributions, value, and accomplishments *today*.

The feedback you received for a job well done … write it down. The email you received praising your contributions in yesterday's meeting/Zoom call … write it down. I also encourage you to keep all positive emails, especially those complimenting you, in a folder. Let's be honest, some days are tough, and we all need positive reinforcement from time to time. I have a folder labeled "Cicely" for emails I receive that lift me up. Starting small also provides the opportunity for you to develop daily, weekly, and monthly habits of tracking this important information.

We've talked a little bit about doubt in these first couple of chapters, and we will spend more time on defeating your doubt in later chapters. For now, know that starting small offers positive reinforcement that you can champion yourself. You can advocate for your success and pull up your chair to the table of success you seek. This is doable. Take it one day at a time to build momentum and positive habits.

When those moments of doubt creep up on you, let your mind go back to the times when you achieved, when you overcame, when you reached the level you wanted to or achieved a goal you set out to accomplish. Remind yourself that you have worked hard to achieve your current position, and you are not going to discount your hard work nor the success that results.

As I said earlier, my father served in Vietnam as a corporal in the US Marine Corp. He was so proud of his service to our country and lived the motto "Once a Marine, always a Marine." He always wore his USMC cap and loved it when someone thanked him for his service.

When my dad passed away suddenly on Easter Sunday 2020, in honor of his service, the funeral home had a throw made with pictures that memorialized who he was. Dad taught me to champion myself throughout my life. When I failed to meet a goal, he would tell me to try again. If I wanted to conquer the world one day, he would say I could do it. When I lost my job, he asked if I was okay, then immediately directed me to figure out what was next.

None of us are immune to doubt. How you defeat your doubt, and how you respond to those moments, will change as you become more comfortable championing yourself and reinforcing your self-respect and self-worth. As one person said to me after a coaching session, "Wow, I feel really good about myself."

Only you can decide to seek the change you desire.

It is important that you understand that your skills, talents, work ethic, and value make you an asset to any organization you choose to join. If you are wondering why I'm bringing this up now, it is because being true to yourself and being honest with yourself can be challenging. However, it is necessary to confront the single biggest obstacle to your championing yourself and your success: *You!*

Only you can decide to seek the change you desire.

What, Why, How

I want to do some one-on-one coaching with you and give you some practical tools to combat doubt. So roll up your sleeves and grab your computer, iPad, pen and paper, or a blank journal. We will brainstorm together. When you write things down, it is easier to tie your thoughts and examples together.

First of all, I want to help you establish your "what." By that I mean, What is the goal you want to accomplish? What success are you seeking? You may be someone who is already successful in your role, but you want to make even more of an impact. You may be a recent graduate just starting your career, a CEO, or someone in between who is aspiring to get to different levels in an organization. No matter where you are in your career, you have a "what" that you want to accomplish. It is vitally important that you are crystal clear on this, so you can create a practical plan to achieve your "what."

Next, let's focus on your "why." In his bestselling book *Start with Why: How Great Leaders Inspire Everyone to Take Action*, Simon Sinek notes that everyone has a "why." Sinek believes that every person knows what it is they do, that some of us know how we do it, but very few of us have ever really taken the time to think about *why* we do what we do. Yet those who are clear on their "why" are the ones who have never given up and have succeeded.[2] The thing about the "why" is it's so personal, so unique, to each person. Now ask yourself, "Why am I doing what I am doing? Why do I want that promotion? Why do I want more responsibility in my current position? Why do I truly want to advocate for myself?" Look past the words that come

---

2   Nancy A. Ruffin, "Why Having a Strong 'Why' Statement Is the Key to Staying Motivated and Focused," HuffPost, August 8, 2017, https://www.huffpost.com/entry/why-having-a-strong-why-statement-is-the-key-to-staying_b_5983ca40e4b0bd823 202969e.

to mind and search for the inspiration that is in your heart and the desire that drives you to increase your capabilities, your abilities, and your leadership potential.

Finally, let's look at your "how." The C.H.A.I.R. program is all about your "how," and the sweet spot for C.H.A.I.R. Leadership and the five strategies comes into play to provide clarity on your "how." *How* do you get "there" … whatever "there" is for you? *How* do you change the trajectory of your career and life? *How* do you reach the level of success you desire? *How* do you become a true person of impact?

As you get crystal clear about your what, why, and how, these will help you get to the table of success and stay there. Your what, why, and how will greatly enhance your impact and greatly enhance your success.

Practice, Practice, Practice

With your what, why, and how in focus, you'll be able to see how they line up with, and contribute to, your values, contributions, and accomplishments.

I want you to look back over your last week or two, or maybe your last quarter, and list two or three of your personal strengths. Next, write down three positive contributions you have

The road to success is taken one step at a time.

made toward your own growth and development, or that you have made to your team, or that you have made toward your organization. Remember, start small. The road to success is taken one step at a time. If you write down twenty things, that won't be memorable, and you won't be able to keep track of all the details in a way that you can advocate for yourself without coming across as being boastful. Your "*you*" list is something you must be able to keep in your head and be ready to articulate when the time comes.

Once you have your list, practice what you are going to say. Yes, practice. When you first start out, you're not going to get this right, and maybe not even the first couple of times. That's okay. Rehearse your narrative. You do that in front of a mirror, with a friend, or even with your pet—if it will sit still long enough! If you practice regularly, you will be ready to show up differently without fumbling, when the moment presents itself. You will know your stuff!

The goal is to come across as self-assured when championing yourself.

I also encourage you to track your big wins and the incremental progress you are making. Make note of the tactical everyday conversations. Yes, there are those big, strategic moments in your career, such as your quarterly or annual reviews, but this is also about your day-to-day, and how you talk about yourself and your work in daily conversations.

Part of championing yourself is showing up differently by starting to change the words and language you are using—how you are talking about yourself and how you are talking about your work, your values, and your contributions. That's where the real, actionable piece of this comes in.

Pull Up Your C.H.A.I.R.— Action Items

As your coach, I encourage you to take these actions:

- Spend some serious time with yourself and find out what your "what," "why," and "how" are.

- When you have clarity, share these with someone to get their feedback.

- Determine two or three accomplishments that illustrate your value, contribution, or an achievement.

- Practice saying these out loud so that you have the self-assurance to champion yourself.

- Be ready to succinctly recount these when the moment comes.

"H"— HONESTY

A note to my readers:

As your coach, I trust by now that you realize I am on your side. I am your cheerleader, because I know you can do what we have talked about so far. I want you to champion yourself and advocate for yourself to achieve the success you desire.

Now that we have a good rapport, in this section I want to help you take a good look at yourself, which is why the "H" in C.H.A.I.R. stands for honesty—self-honesty. In the following chapters, I want to help you get crystal clear on your weaknesses and potential blind spots, both of which can impede your progress, personal and professional.

I am going to be honest: self-honesty can be tough for some people. I can tell you that throughout my career, confronting my blind spots and diffusing them has been a challenge. However, I've done the necessary work, and continue to do the work, so that I can champion myself with integrity.

We all have strengths. We all have weaknesses. The key is to turn those weaknesses into strengths. Or at the very least, have strategies to deal with them, including minimizing their power and sway.

As we move forward, I want you to be brutally honest with yourself—that is what championing yourself requires. Self-honesty compels you to acknowledge and confront areas of your personality that you would rather not deal with. It would be a disservice to you and your desire to grow and lead yourself if you don't take the time for self-reflection.

If you recall from the preface, I made this statement and asked you to repeat it: "If you can't lead yourself, you can't lead others."

> **We all have strengths. We all have weaknesses. The key is to turn those weaknesses into strengths.**

Leading yourself starts with being honest with yourself, and being honest with yourself will force you to confront something we all have: self-deception.

Self-deception is the inability to see that we have a problem, a weakness.

Of all the problems in organizations, self-deception is the most common and most damaging. Being honest means that you must confront your own self-deception, blind spots, and weaknesses and put a plan in place to deal with them.

Now get ready to dig into self-honesty and self-deception, and to do the hard work you need to do to champion yourself from a foundation of self-honesty and integrity!

CHAPTER

4

YOU'VE GOT SOME WORK TO DO

ACKNOWLEDGING YOUR WEAKNESSES

That which we persist in doing becomes easier to do—not that the nature of the thing has changed, but that our power to do has increased.
—RALPH WALDO EMERSON

Before you dive into this chapter, take a deep breath. Maybe two deep breaths.

Whether it is your professional or personal life, it's easy to acknowledge the parts of your personality that others like, but nothing is harder than acknowledging the parts of your personality that others don't like.

I chose the word "honesty" for the "H" in C.H.A.I.R. because honesty with yourself and about yourself will make or break your career. I have learned these lessons the hard way, and this is the toughest strategy I teach.

When I talk about weaknesses, I am also going to use the term "blind spots." Please know that I do not mean to be offensive to anyone who is visually impaired when I use this phrase. I experience visual impairment. I use this phrase to describe the negative personality traits we have that we may not acknowledge *or* realize their impact.

I'll use myself as an illustration, because it is easier for me to talk about my shortfalls than someone else's. Like I said, I have learned the hard way.

I had never taken a 360 review before I started working in the private sector. Congressional offices rarely employ these types of assessment and feedback mechanisms. These kinds of reviews can be brutal; let's acknowledge that right now. These reviews ask for anonymous, objective input about you, giving your boss, your colleagues, and peers the opportunity to point out your blind spots or weaknesses—can you say ouch?

I remember a 360 assessment I took when I was at Dunkin'. The feedback I received from my peers was mostly positive. They loved working with me; I was a high performer, etc. However, the feedback said I needed to be more vulnerable with my colleagues and allow people to get to know me. The feedback also said that I leave dead bodies in my wake.

Wait, what? Who, me?

My first reaction was to figure out who wrote those comments. How dare they say that about me! They had to be wrong.

When I reviewed my results with my boss, she reaffirmed those comments but in a much nicer way. She explained that I am not that way with her, but she could see how I interact with others. I was so

> **Results are great, but how you get results makes a difference.**

busy getting the job done, I didn't care what it took to get the results. She explained that when people get to know me, like she knows me, and when I take the time to get to know them, the feedback will be different and my process for collaboration will be different. I realized I had to be honest with myself: results are great, but how you get results makes a difference.

Corporate America taught me a lot of lessons, and this lesson I was thankful for.

Self-Honesty, Self-Reflection

I want you to think about what the word "honesty" means to you. How do you define honesty? How do you display honesty in your life? Do you champion yourself through honesty? If you think about it, when most people talk about honesty, they are referring to telling the truth. However, the honesty I am talking about is being real with yourself and with others about who you are, what you want, and what you need to do to champion yourself with integrity. This is called "self-honesty."

Self-honesty sharpens your focus on who you truly are and how you impact others. And when you are honest with yourself, it allows you to observe everything around you with clarity.

Self-honesty starts with "self-reflection."

Self-reflection is looking into a mirror and describing what you see—not what you see on the outside, but what you see on the inside. The word "reflection" means to contemplate something, and in this case you are going to contemplate yourself. Why is this important? Self-reflection leads to self-awareness where you are willing to take a hard look at your thoughts, feelings, emotions, and actions with objectivity. This is why I previously addressed not making excuses; if you are going to be honest with yourself and have objective self-reflection, then you can't make excuses for your words or behavior.

Objective self-reflection allows you to look at yourself with interest and curiosity—without self-criticism. It allows you to dig deeper, to question your very being: Why do I feel this way? Why do I do what I do? Why do I come across in a particular way that seems to turn others off? These are the types of questions that objectivity allows us to ask that lead to self-honesty.

Leadership and Self-Deception

One pitfall that many leaders fall into is that of self-deception. Self-deception can be defined as lying to yourself or making yourself believe something that isn't really true. It is the practice of convincing yourself to believe something that is actually false. Leaders who are self-deceived create a breach in trust, and trust is foundational to all leadership levels.

Leaders can be their own biggest obstacle to success. Seldom does a leader make time to be introspective and to see through objective eyes if they are the source of a problem. How does this happen? As you think about your leadership skills and potential, I want you to consider this: leadership and self-deception is the idea that the leader acts one way, but they are actually perceived in a completely different way. Now ask yourself, "Does this definition apply to me?"

In their book *Leadership and Self-Deception*, the Arbinger Institute states:[3]

> [Self-deception] blinds us to the true causes of problems, and once we are "blind," all the solutions we can think of will actually make matters worse. Whether at work or at home, self-deception obscures the truth about ourselves, corrupts our views of others and ourselves, and inhibits our ability to make wise and helpful decisions. To the extent we are self-deceived, both our happiness and our leadership are undermined at every turn ...

I would add this to the above: to the extent we are self-deceived, our happiness, *our self-leadership*, and our team leadership are undermined at every turn.

Where to Start

In addressing self-deception, the first place to start is with your own mindset. Are you mentally ready to do the work necessary? Are you prepared to look past your defenses and excuses?

Remember, your mindset matters! You have to be mentally prepared to be gut-honest. If you are not in this place, then take some time to get there; don't move on until you are ready—but don't do yourself a disservice by taking too long to get there.

---

3   The Arbinger Institute, *Leadership and Self-Deception: Getting Out of the Box*, Oakland: Berrett-Koehler Publishers, September 2018.

It is impossible to be honest with yourself and be self-reflective by trying to keep everything in your mind. That's why I encouraged you earlier to start a self-reflection journal, electronic or a physical book. Now, write down the following:

- What are your blind spots? Blind spots are character weaknesses that we cannot or will not acknowledge. Even on the off chance that we do recognize or admit to a character flaw, we will come up with a creative reason—which is simply an excuse—as to why it is part of our lives. Be honest! Don't allow self-deception to blind you.

- I'm sure that some of you are asking, "I really don't know my blind spots, so what do I do?" Feel free to ask someone who cares enough about you to be honest with you. If you choose to do this, then be willing to thank that person for their honesty—and don't hold it against them. If asking someone else is a step too far for you at this point, consider reviewing past performance reviews, 360 assessments, and any other feedback mechanisms for this information.

- How do others perceive you? Do they see you as bold and brash? Calm and peaceful? Wise? Impetuous? Deceitful? A gossiper? If you're unsure, feel free to ask someone—but be sure to ask someone who will be honest with you. Is their perception a reality?

- Now ask yourself, "Is the way others see me the way I truly am?"

If you are struggling to know your blind spots, here is the top ten list from *Inc.* magazine:[4]

1. Going it alone (being afraid to ask for help)

2. Being insensitive of your behavior on others (being unaware of how you show up)

3. Having an "I know" attitude (valuing being right above everything else)

4. Avoiding the difficult conversations (conflict avoidance)

5. Blaming others or circumstances (playing the victim; refusing responsibility)

6. Treating commitments casually (not honoring the other person's time, energy, resources)

7. Conspiring against others (driven by a personal agenda)

8. Withholding emotional commitment (emotional blackmail)

9. Not taking a stand (lack of commitment to a position)

10. Tolerating "good enough" (low standards for performance)

Being honest about your blind spots will give you a high-level perspective of yourself.

I've shared one story about my blind spots. Here are a couple of others.

I am impatient. I want things done—now! I can be impatient with myself and with others. Even though I know this about myself, there are times when it sneaks up on me, and I become impatient before I even realize it. When I sense impatience rising up inside of

---

4   Marissa Levin, "The Top 10 Leadership Blind Spots, and 5 Ways to Turn Them into Strengths," *Inc.*, July 13, 2017, https://www.inc.com/marissa-levin/the-top-10-leadership-blind-spots-and-5-ways-to-tu.html.

me, I have to make a conscious decision *not* to speak from what I'm feeling, because what I am really doing is projecting my values, my work ethic, onto the other person. I need to take a deep breath and realize that others might not process as quickly as I do, or they may not move as fast as I do. I need to separate myself from the other person and still be me, while allowing them to be themselves.

I am not okay with just being okay. I don't settle for mediocre, nor do I deal with laziness very well. When I see these traits in others, I just don't understand that mentality. Do you want to be successful and a person of impact? Then just being okay is not okay and won't get you there.

I am a very direct communicator. Very direct. I never mean to be harsh, but I don't beat around the bush either. This is how we were raised in our family, and that military mentality has been instilled in my brother and me. Now, that is a good thing because I am clear about what I am saying and why I am saying it. Usually, people tell me that they like people who shoot straight, so they know where they stand. The truth is people say this, but most don't really mean it. When they are on the receiving end of honest feedback, they complain that I am too harsh and too mean. My blind spot in my communication style comes in the way I "land on people." I will talk more about this in chapter 5, but in essence what I am saying is that by being direct, it is easy to come across as uncaring, lacking compassion or empathy, etc.

I am a very disciplined person. I will go the extra mile when no one else wants to, and I know that is a great trait to have.

How is that a blind spot, you may ask?

Others can interpret my standards as being too high—too high for them. As a result, I don't tolerate poor performers well who don't care about their work product. Their lackadaisical attitude can negatively impact others.

Being disciplined also creates confidence. However, confidence is often perceived as arrogance. And to be honest, I have been called arrogant and a lot worse. When I champion and advocate for myself, I let others know that I am disciplined, and I am confident that I provide value. I don't apologize for my strong work ethic.

As you read this list, you may think, *How are these blind spots if she knows them?* They are no longer blind spots for me, because I acknowledge them and deal with them. However, at one time each of these traits was pointed out to me by someone else—that's when true self-reflection reveals I need to acknowledge, own, and minimize these traits.

Now that I've been honest with you, I would like you to get honest with yourself. In your journal, write down the following:

- What are your weaknesses? For instance, do you work well with others or leave others in the wake behind you?

- Do you truly engage others on projects or simply give them lip service?

- Do you claim all the accolades, or can you include others in your successes?

- Do you have trouble saying no to people?

- Do you struggle to ask others for help?

- Do you tend to get "lost in the details" of a project?

- Are you too busy creating visions and scenarios in your mind that you cannot quantify what you want to do?

If you are impatient, write that down. If you are a direct communicator, it can be both a strength and blind spot. Write it down. You don't tolerate certain personality types well? You got it ... write it down. Start making the list, and you can always add to or take things off later.

After you identify your weaknesses, prioritize in your journal the most important areas you need to work on, keeping in mind that if you're going to champion your strengths, you have got to be gut-honest about your weaknesses. Remember, this is not a list of self-criticisms; it is a list that will benefit you in the long run. Even if you can easily write them down, confronting parts of your personality that can hinder your advancement is not easy.

To advance in your career, you have to be open to change. Be open to changing your behaviors.

Be open minded that everyone has areas of improvement. You'll be able to determine how to minimize and deal with your weaknesses or any perceived obstacles that you may put in your own way. Don't discount this exercise or neglect doing the self-reflection required to succeed.

Minimizing Your Weaknesses

This is where you can truly begin to champion your "inner self." This is *not* where you make excuses or justify your character deficits or behaviors. Instead, you grow to the place where these no longer impact your life. Determining how to minimize your weaknesses will prepare you for the times when they come to the forefront. You will immediately have strategies and tactics to minimize any negative impact.

Success starts in the mind before it ever manifests itself in life.

There are many ways to minimize your weaknesses, but you first have to acknowledge that you've got some work to do.

Success starts in the mind before it ever manifests itself in life. When your attitude is negative and unproductive, you must *choose* to shift from negative thought patterns. You need to be your own internal coach and give yourself a mental kick in the butt, then champion yourself by charging forward with power, conviction, and faith. Here are a few tactics to ensure a positive mindset:

✔ Determine incentives

Ask yourself, "What motivates me to take action?" What are you currently doing that makes you want to get out of bed and seize the day? Perhaps you're in a not-so-good place in your mind: What can you do to change your mindset? Give yourself incentives; when you incentivize your mind, you'll incentivize your life.

✔ Set benchmarks

Select mental benchmarks to help you visualize goals as you strive to grow and develop. This type of mental practice keeps your attitude positive and directed toward your success.

✔ Manage anxiety

When challenges surface, it is easy to lose control of your thoughts and feelings. When the inevitable challenges come, stay clear of catastrophic thinking (i.e., *I'm going to fail, and my entire world will fall apart*) and resist the temptation to go down the "What if?" slippery slope of anxiety.

Anxiety is fear of the unknown projected forward. Remind yourself that a "What if?" is not happening in your present situation; it is simply a story that your mind is making up. Maintain a positive mindset by focusing on what you can control right now, and train yourself to focus on solutions, not problems.

✔ Get hungry

Are you hungry for success? If the answer is yes, it will permeate all that you are doing. It will show up in your can-do attitude, and that you are committed to achieving what you set out to do. Remember, total commitment cuts through doubt; anything less is a sellout.

✔ Be lighthearted

Don't drive yourself so hard that you miss out on the fun side of life. Find humor and be willing to poke fun at yourself. You are not perfect, nor will you ever be. Enjoy the journey you are on.

✔ Aim for self-mastery

Self-beliefs control thoughts, thoughts control feelings, and feelings control actions and reactions. Thus, your mindset is controlled by two things: your self-beliefs and your thoughts. If you are naturally more pessimistic, take responsibility for consciously selecting a glass-half-full mentality. Choose to fight against what you know internally is holding you down. Pessimism and optimism are attitudes we choose, and the one you choose will go a long way toward determining your immediate and long-term success. Remember this mantra: attitude is everything. If you believe you can succeed, you have the foundation for success.

Once you have a positive mindset about your self-honesty, the question then becomes, "How do I minimize my weaknesses?"

The ultimate tactic to minimizing your weaknesses is to *proactively* acknowledge them. In the past, when I have started a new role, I have proactively told my team, "I am a direct communicator. Please know that I am not trying to be harsh. Before you say you like direct communication, please know that most people don't when they are on the receiving end of honest feedback." I also say, "I am very impatient when deadlines are missed, so please meet project deadlines or communicate in advance if you are going to miss the deadline."

Acknowledge them, own them, determine what you want to do about them, and move on. When you acknowledge and take ownership of your blind spots, not only are you taking responsibility, you also take away someone else's power to penalize you for those weaknesses.

That last part is key.

When you acknowledge and own the parts of your personality that you need to work on, you minimize someone else's ability to ding you for these weaknesses and blind spots.

I want to digress for a moment to share a critical piece of advice for your career and leadership journey.

Acknowledgment and ownership are traits of true leaders and true professionals. One compliment I have always received from my bosses was that I acknowledged and owned my mistakes, and the mistakes of my team, whenever they occurred. When a mistake or error happened—whether others knew about it or not—before my boss could say a word, I always acknowledged the mistake, told my boss that I owned it and that it would be corrected. It is easy to blame others and create excuses. It is much harder to take ownership. Now that I am a business owner and entrepreneur, I do the same with my clients and stakeholders. Acknowledgment and ownership will serve you well in all facets of your professional journey.

Now, take a good look in the mirror and ask yourself, "Am I willing to do the self-reflection needed to ensure my success? Am I willing to be honest with myself and others? How can I start acknowledging and owning my weaknesses in order to minimize them?" If you truly want to grow, if you truly want to face your blind spots and find out what you need to work on, then there is only one answer: Yes!

Practice, Practice, Practice

Practice makes perfect, which is why you consistently see this section in each of the five strategies.

When you practice, you figure out ways to minimize the impact of your blind spots and weaknesses. You are honest with yourself about your strengths and weaknesses and know how to use them to your advantage.

Self-awareness can be a huge attribute, if used correctly. That's another reason I want you to keep a self-reflection journal. It will help you acknowledge your blind spots, determine how to minimize their impact, and move on. That way, you are comfortable with the strengths you know you have, and you can be comfortable with your blind spots as well. This is vitally important.

If you don't want to proactively acknowledge blind spots or perceived problems, you will take a reactive approach when someone mentions them. And being reactive instead of proactive is never a good thing. It is easy to get defensive when someone else is pointing out your weaknesses to you. Whatever you do, *don't* get defensive. Even if the person doesn't approach you the right way, take a deep breath, count to ten, or do whatever you need to do to *not* respond defensively. You could say, "Thank you for your input," then walk away, so you can process what was said. Reacting when you are emotionally triggered will only lead to actions you will regret later.

Trust me, not keeping my cool was one of my weaknesses and used to be a blind spot until I tackled it. I did this by admitting and acknowledging that I have a short fuse. My mouth can get me into trouble, and I have zero tolerance for certain types of people. I prepare myself beforehand by knowing who I am interacting with and how I perceive that person. I acknowledge it, so that I am prepared for if and when this weakness crops up. Again, proactive acknowledgment is always better than reactive explanation.

Here is a great way to deal with a blind spot: acknowledge and frame the conversation on your terms, not someone else's terms. For instance, if I want a promotion or new role, I might say, "I believe I am a good fit for this role; I am a good team player, I lead teams well, and I am looking forward to identifying opportunities to enhance the team's work and impact. Now, while I am excited and ready to take on a new role, I know I have some work to do on being more patient with team members." I just minimized my impatience.

It is a simple three-step process: acknowledge, diffuse and minimize, and move on.

This takes time and effort. You have to know yourself and your style. You have to decide which approach works best for you.

As we close this chapter, I'd like to encourage you with these words:

Whenever you find yourself doubting how far you can go, just remember how far you have come. Remember everything you have faced. All of the battles you have won, and all of the fears you have overcome.
—ANONYMOUS

Pull Up Your C.H.A.I.R.— Action Items

As your coach, I encourage you to take these actions:

- If you have a journal, now is the time to start your self-reflection. If you don't have a journal, then start one electronically or purchase a blank notebook.

- What are your two or three greatest weaknesses?

- What is your plan to overcome or minimize them?

- If you find your self-reflection or honesty waning, how can you motivate yourself to keep going?

CHAPTER

5

KNOW HOW YOU LAND ON PEOPLE

HOW TO BE HONEST WITH YOURSELF

Just be honest with yourself. That opens the door.
—VERNON HOWARD

As I noted earlier, I am a direct communicator. Just like all good sports and business coaches, I prefer clear channels of communication—no fluff, no beating around bushes.

I recently gave a virtual speech about C.H.A.I.R. Leadership in which I acknowledged that I'm a direct communicator. I also stated the downside of direct communication: people say they love the honesty, but in their feedback I'm told that I am too harsh. Then I said to the audience, "We're always told to be honest and candid, but when you're honest and candid, you get pinged for it." I was pleasantly surprised when the chat box started filling up with "I get that all the time!" and "I'm with you on that!"

Sure, it was great to have people agree with me, but I have learned the hard way that my words may come across as harsh and biting, and really penetrating to someone, even if I don't mean them to. Because I was raised as a "little Marine," I know that Marines don't suffer fools lightly. They say what they mean and mean what they say. And so do I.

The really tough piece of this, though, is that I had to acknowledge there were many times when I came across as harsh, even uncaring. I didn't mean it that way, but that's still how I was being perceived.

I will always be a direct communicator, but I continually work on being direct and framing it in such a way that others can receive from me.

That's why you have to know how you land on people.

You might have been thinking, *Know how you land on people … What does that mean?* How you "land" on people means how you come across to them, how others perceive you. If you want to know how you are landing on others, ask yourself two questions: "How do I present myself?" and "How do others perceive me?"

You may not agree, but as your coach I'm telling you this is key based on my experience and the feedback I have received and given throughout my career.

Before you read on, I encourage you to take a few minutes and complete the following "how you come across" assessment: https://www.psychologies.co.uk/test-how-do-you-come-across. What I like about this is that you'll get immediate feedback.

Whether you perceive a behavior or personality trait as an obstacle is something you have to decide for yourself. Quite frankly, even if you don't think it is an obstacle, you still have to know how you land on people. If you land negatively and that is your reputation, then it is an obstacle to your progress.

When I first started getting negative feedback about my communication style, I could have gotten defensive, or I could have taken a good, hard look in the mirror and seen how I was landing on people, then made necessary adjustments. I chose the latter, and that's when I read the book *Leadership and Self-Deception*, by the Arbinger

Don't give them a reason to say no.

Institute. I chose to take a hard look at myself, because I truly wanted to champion myself by becoming a better person and a more empathic communicator. Even though I made this decision years ago, I am still aware of my tendencies, and I am always careful to understand how I *want* to land on people … then I make sure I come across that way. And if I don't? I simply acknowledge my error, make the necessary change on the spot, and move on.

The other reason you must consider the way you land on people is that you don't want to give your team, your stakeholders, or your audience a reason to deny your request. Don't give them a reason to say no. If you give people a justification to say no, oftentimes they will take it rather than have a hard conversation and taking a good look at what you have to say.

Practical Strategies

Perhaps you are like me, a direct communicator. Or maybe you're the type of person who would not raise your hand, even if your life depended on it. I'm not telling you to change who you are, because then you wouldn't be showing up in an authentic way. But how do you "couch" what you're saying? How do you say what you want/need to say in a way that others receive it, without them casting stones your way? The point isn't to go all the way to the other extreme to try to change your personality. The point is to take actionable, doable steps that can minimize your weaknesses. And remember, start small.

When I coach clients about self-honesty, communication is one of the top two challenges that come up. Some people are direct and get told they're harsh. Other people are told they need to speak up more. Everybody is somewhere on that communication spectrum. Now is the time to work on your communication skills.

A quick note: if you have been procrastinating through the last chapter and haven't started thinking about your self-honesty, then it is time to start. Go back over chapter 4 before continuing with this chapter. However, if you have been doing what I've asked you to do, then you can move on.

The Basics

This may sound obvious, but at the outset the really tough piece of this is that you have to acknowledge how you come across, even if you don't mean it that way, because that's still how you are being perceived. For instance, for people who are less confident and have a lot of self-doubt, being taken to task by a direct communicator can absolutely cripple them. I've seen it in my career, and I've done it in my career, and I've had to apologize for it. I've had to, quite frankly, learn to soften my words to be more tactical.

Now, in your self-reflection journal, write down what you *know* about how you land on people, then write about how you *want* to land on people. Remember, this exercise isn't just for the straight shooters. It's also for those who are too timid to speak up and for everyone in between. Yes, there are times when we all land on people wrong. If you are having trouble with this, then go back to your list of blind spots and weaknesses, and you will come up with ample illustrations of how you are coming across to others.

> **How you land on people is when perception becomes reality, whether you realize it or not.**

You have to know how your words are perceived and how your actions are perceived. Because how you land on people is when perception becomes reality, whether you realize it or not.

I have been coaching someone who lands on people the wrong way all the time. He was close to termination when we started working together. I could tell his communication style was undermining his success, so that is where we started our work together. His style came across as statements of fact, negative and judgmental. That wasn't his intent; he thought he was communicating his opinion. I am coaching him to express his opinion—whether based on professional expertise or personal experiences—but to think about the words he is using. There are many words he could use. The key is to work on language choices and softening language, so that he isn't immediately discounted or ignored because his message is received wrong.

Your Approach

In chapter 4, I noted that you can have a proactive approach or a reactive approach. Now it's time to choose your approach and be confident in your choice. A proactive approach focuses on eliminating problems before they arise. A reactive approach responds to events after they have happened. The difference between these two is the perspective they provide.

A proactive approach includes the following:

- Self-direction: you state or demonstrate how you will add value, minimize a problem, etc., without being told to do so.

- Managing expectations: you clearly state what you can/cannot or will/will not do. For example, you keep your manager regularly informed of what you are doing and what needs to be completed.

- Anticipating objections: you think about issues or problems someone may bring up and determine what you will say/do.

- Practice and rehearse: you think about what you want to say and why you want to say it. Then you rehearse these points, so that you are fully prepared.

A reactive approach includes the following:

- Minimization: you bring whatever problem is presented into perspective (i.e., the department will not fall apart if the copier dies).

- Contingency: you are flexible to adapt to ever-changing expectations or demands.

- Reassurance: you let others know that you understand what is needed and meet expectations.

- Open-mindedness: you hear what others say and have a willingness to adopt their ideas/suggestions/directions.

- Feedback: you wait for feedback about your weaknesses or blind spots.

- Reactions: you react defensively when feedback about your weaknesses and blind spots occurs.

The approach you choose is the one that suits you best—and you can certainly choose to combine them, if the situation demands it. However, there is a third approach: you can ignore this chapter and take your chances. Just realize that if you choose to ignore the strategies in this chapter—and in this book—you do so at your own peril.

Getting Feedback

If you really want to be honest with yourself, then be courageous and ask others for feedback on how you can grow and improve. However, you are not looking for general feedback—"You did a great job!" You are looking for *constructive* feedback. This means you are asking for issue-focused feedback, rather than someone's values-based or personal judgment founded on their personal views, attitude, or motivation. For instance, you may want to give better presentations, speak in a calmer manner, voice your opinion in a positive way, etc. Feedback can be given verbally or written. But be prepared to remain objective; you cannot take what others say personally.

I recently read a great article that helped me crystalize why feedback was so important. In the article, author Shankar Vedantam noted that:[5]

> When we go through vulnerable times, we need to reach out to other people. When other people are going through vulnerable times, we need to reach out to them. In some ways, that idea is at the core of [the book *Useful Delusions: The Power and Paradox of the Self-Deceiving Brain*]—when we see the delusions of other people, it's easy to sit in judgment of them. It's easy to be contemptuous of them. But it is far more helpful and far wiser to be empathetic to them, to be compassionate, and to be curious about how it is they came to be thinking the way they do.

If you are willing to ask for feedback, that means you are willing to be vulnerable, to be transparent. Being vulnerable keeps us all humble. And without humility, it is easy to sit in judgment of others.

When getting feedback, be sure to focus on these:

- Note your response to what is being said and the other person's response when they are talking. Trust your instincts to read how the person feels (body language, facial expressions) when they are giving you feedback.

- Acknowledge any/all feedback, negative or positive.

- Take time to reflect on what you are told, and don't dismiss anything.

---

5   Raju Narisetti, interview with Shankar Vedantam, "Author Talks: Shankar Vedantam on the Power and Paradox of Self-Deception," McKinsey & Company, May 27, 2021, https://www.mckinsey.com/featured-insights/mckinsey-on-books/author-talks-shankar-vedantam-on-the-power-and-paradox-of-self-deception.

When Blind Spots Reemerge

While working through this book, please keep one thing in mind: you are a work in progress!

I want you to repeat that: "I am a work in progress." Now, take a sticky note and post this mantra on your computer or on your bathroom mirror so you are reminded every day. You will make mistakes. Your blind spots will reemerge. The more you are aware of your negative tendencies and how you land on people, the more you can minimize these behaviors or work around them.

What do you do when blind spots reemerge? To use a sports phrase, "You have to readjust." That may sound simple, but think about this: in any game, both teams are constantly readjusting to each other on the fly in real time. You have to do the same. If you tend to get lost in the details of a project, and you're working on being strategic instead of tactical, there are times when you will slip back into old patterns. As soon as you notice this, readjust. Take whatever steps you need to and move on.

I've told you that I am impatient and can have a short fuse. Even though I have been working on this for many years, on rare occasions I still lose my cool. What do I do during these times? I take my own advice—I get gut-honest with myself, and I make the changes I need to make. Then I move on.

I also like what author and speaker Brian Tracy has to say: "All airplanes are off course 99 percent of the time. The purpose and role of the pilot and the avionics is to continually bring the plane back on course so that it arrives on schedule at its destination."[6] You are the pilot of your life; don't let your blind spots cause you to lose track of

---

6   Brian Tracy, "Making Course Corrections," Brian Tracy International, https://www.briantracy.com/blog/brians-words-of-wisdom/making-course-corrections/.

where you are, what you want to do, how you want to get there, and how you are championing yourself. Just like the pilots, you need to keep yourself on course.

Please hear me on this: the worst thing you can do is to get down on yourself and take on a defeatist mentality. Every champion in any arena—from business to sports—has been knocked down a few times. But every champion has the fortitude to get back up, dust themselves off, readjust, and get back in the game. Your goal is to champion yourself the same way. When you slip back into old habits, ask yourself, "What do I want to do at this point?" Your answer will go a long way in determining how you are going to show up differently in the future, and your level of fortitude for doing so.

Pull Up Your C.H.A.I.R.— Action Items

As your coach, I encourage you to take these actions:

- Maintain your self-reflection journal on a regular basis about current situations you are in.

- What blind spot reoccurs on a regular basis?

- In your journal, create a plan or method that will help you to readjust.

- If you aren't doing this already, ask others for constructive feedback on a regular basis.

CHAPTER

6

STAY TRUE TO YOURSELF

THE ROAD AHEAD

Don't limit yourself. Many people limit themselves to what they think
they can do. You can go as far as your mind lets you.
What you believe, remember, you can achieve.
—MARY KAY ASH

As you read this chapter, I want you to think about a pilot flying a plane. It is heading in a particular direction, but because of the air current, clouds, and other factors, the pilot needs to "keep course correcting" in order to maintain the plane's heading and reach its destination.

You are the captain of your life, and it is up to you to keep course correcting who you are and what you are doing, in order to champion yourself and reach your destination (i.e., a promotion, a new position, or career change, etc.).

One of the ways you can keep course correcting is by recognizing when you have gone off course by not being honest with yourself or by letting self-deception creep in, then determining what you need to do to get back on course.

Another way you can keep course correcting is by understanding something called "projection." I want to make a distinction here. In the previous chapters, I noted that how you "land" on people means how you come across to them, how others perceive you. Projection, however, is about how you put your views, opinions, and judgments onto others and expect them to see and do things the way you do. If you want to lead yourself, if you want to champion yourself, then you need to understand how you "project" yourself onto other people and what to do about it.

Think of a projector, a machine designed to project whatever input it receives onto a screen for everyone to see. Perhaps you've never thought of this, but we are all like projectors. We project what is inside of us—how we think, feel, or act—onto other people, and we are dumbfounded and disappointed when they don't act or react like we do. We think, *Why would you think that way? Why would you respond or react the way you did?* We might also think downright nasty thoughts: *Are you an idiot? Are you stupid?*

What is happening in these situations? We are shocked that other people are actually different than we are; each is their own person with different thoughts, feelings, actions, and reactions than we have. Now, that may sound obvious to your rational mind, but on a subconscious level this is not rational at all.

I have a surprise for you.

Other people rarely think, feel, or act like we do.

Please think about what I just said as you move through this chapter. Why? Because it will help you to keep course correcting.

For instance, impatience tends to be one of the big blind spots for many people. One way it keeps coming up is when we are impatient with people who don't meet deadlines. We've all been there, and this is a pet peeve of mine. I don't have a lot of patience for people who miss deadlines and people who put work on me because they didn't do their part. A colleague who doesn't meet a deadline affects everyone else. A boss who continually misses meetings is holding their team back, but no one is willing to say anything. Impatience can pop up when people don't do what they're supposed to be doing, creating an emergency for everybody. When I'm impatient, the unspoken message I am sending is "I don't miss deadlines. I don't put my work on others, and you shouldn't either."

Other people rarely think, feel, or act like we do.

For example, impatience is a common way we project ourselves onto people. When we are impatient, we tend toward gossip and/or passive-aggressive behavior, such as giving the cold shoulder, holding a grudge, or being resentful, all of which can easily spiral into something worse and can definitely destroy a relationship—or a career.

Another way impatience pops up is for those who make decisions very quickly versus people who want to think about it and get back to you. But what happens when you don't have days for someone to process their thoughts? If you're in a meeting and need to make a decision on the spot, you need the feedback—now.

"Can't I think about it and come back to you?"

"No! I need it now."

Think about this scenario, or something similar that you have seen or experienced, and I'm sure you'll see how "projection" plays a major role in any disconnect.

Especially during the early part of my career, I would let my impatience land on people. My impatience was generated by my thought, *I move at a fast pace; everyone else should too.* After multiple people told me that I think and move faster than others, I had to think about their comments and how I project myself onto others. I had to be honest with myself and realize how I was being perceived, even if I didn't intend to come across that way. Then I had to figure out how to soften my approach, practice patience, and realize I needed to give people time to process information and reach their own conclusion.

I had to be aware of when impatience was rising up inside of me. Then I had to ask myself, "What is happening that is making me impatient? What am I reacting to? How do I want to handle this differently so that I'm not projecting myself onto others and land on people in a way they can receive from me?" At first this seemed very mechanical, but now it is second nature.

I want to pause for a moment and ask you to think about something. In the same article I referenced in chapter 5, author Shankar Vedantam notes:

> The great physicist and scientist Richard Feynman said, "The first rule in science is that you must not fool yourself, and you are the easiest person to fool." Think about this important insight. All of us believe that other people are prone to self-deception. The very nature of self-deception makes it very hard for us to see when we ourselves are its victims. [7]

This is such a provoking thought! If we don't keep course correcting, we can quickly and easily fall into self-deception. Self-deception causes us to be blind to our blind spots, and we no longer acknowledge them, or, worse, we start making excuses for our poor attitudes and behavior. When this happens, we stop growing and changing.

Here's another blind spot of mine. I am always assertive ... but, at times, too assertive. Some would even call me aggressive.

When I have a goal and know what I'm going after, I am fully focused. I also know that, in DC, aggressiveness wins, and when you're not aggressive, you get run over by the herd. When a client hires me and asks, "What's my strategy?" I move fast because I know what their goal is, and I know how to get them there. I usually jump right in and start putting the plans together. I'm thinking, *You can sit back and be passive and wait for things to come your way, or you can aggressively take the reins and really control the outcome of what you're seeking.* However, I have to guard against expecting my client to think and act the same way.

When I'm onboarding a new client or a new project, I tell them up front that I can be assertive in my communication and actions. "We're going to take an aggressive approach to what you want to

---

7   Raju Narisetti, interview with Shankar Vedantam.

accomplish and keep an aggressive timeline, but we can get it done."
I also own my behavior. I say, "I really look forward to working with
you; we're going to get a lot done, and this is going to be great. But
sometimes I can be a little too direct. If that happens, I apologize in
advance."

Then I ask, "Is that okay with you?" A yes means we continue
to stay the course. I think, *Yes! We are on the same page. We have the
same mindset.* But if there is any hesitation, I need to course correct
and be aware if I'm projecting myself onto this person. Perhaps they
need to think things through (something I don't normally need to do).
Maybe they feel overwhelmed but don't want to say so (I'm always
willing to speak up). At this point, I slow myself down and take time
to get to know where they are coming from, what they are thinking,
and what they want. As I learn about my client, I can keep course
correcting. My point is, I don't want to project myself in a way that
turns someone off.

My goal is to proactively acknowledge who I am ahead of
time—I'm saying, "This is who I am"—versus "projecting" myself
and assuming the other person is just like me. And I give the other
person permission to tell me if I'm being too direct, too harsh. I tell
all my business clients and my coaching clients, "I'm here to help
you. Your success is my success. And sometimes I may be a little more
direct than you want me to be, but that's why we're here learning and
partnering together."

If people aren't used to my type of personality, they can easily
be turned off. And if they are new to something, such as working
with the government, the "guns a-blazing" approach might shock
them. But in my world, this is the way you have to be. You have to
be assertive. You have to know who you are working for. It's my job
to explain the environment we are working in. If I don't explain the

need for assertiveness and being proactive, my client(s) are going to be completely turned off, not only by my approach but also perhaps by my tone of voice and the way I'm speaking to them. Assertiveness is good in terms of getting things done, but if I don't realize when and how I am projecting myself onto my client(s), I can land on them in a negative way.

When you course correct, you must be self-aware, you must practice self-honesty, and you must recognize self-deception. It is also extremely important to recognize there are different personality types, and people think, feel, and process differently, such as quick versus slow decision makers in my previous example. The latter want to ponder and reflect, while you might be good at thinking on your feet. However, if you recognize impatience as a blind spot and weakness, then you need to acknowledge that your clients and/or colleagues are different from you—and allow them to be who they are.

Remember, the goal is not to change your personality. And the goal is not to change someone else's personality to match yours. The goal is to understand yourself and your colleagues and realize that your frustration with them, or theirs with you, is born from the fact that you approach things very differently. Neither one of you is right or wrong; you're just different from each other.

I've already provided a few examples of self-reflection. Now, I want you to practice self-reflection as well.

Choose one of your blind spots and write out a time when it came into play. What was the scenario? Who was involved? How did you feel during the situation, and what was the outcome? If you could go through the situation again, how would you approach it differently, now that you understand about projection?

Just to be clear, this information is for you and you alone. You don't need to share this with anyone.

When Others Project onto You

No matter what situation you are in, or whom you are interacting with, there's a good chance that the other person is projecting their thoughts and feelings onto you. This means there is a constant back-and-forth projection in which each person wants the other to act and react like they do. When you think about it, that sounds crazy!

> Be willing to separate yourself from what you feel is being projected by the other person.

Here are some steps you can take when you think or feel someone is projecting onto you:

1. *Recognition.* Recognition of what is happening is the first and most important step. Be aware of the word "*you*" in the other person's conversation. "You should do this or that (because I would do it). You should or shouldn't feel that way (because I don't feel that way)." When you become aware of the "*you*" statements, it is important to ask yourself if there is any truth in what they are saying; this is a big part of being honest with yourself. But always be willing to separate yourself from what you feel is being projected by the other person … this is a huge part of championing yourself.

2. *Their point of view.* Understanding the other person's point of view takes practice and shows emotional maturity. Do your best to stay objective and try to see and understand matters from their point of view. Do you sense some insecurity? Fear? Worry? Doing this will help you understand the other person better and will keep you from getting caught up in your own defenses. Remain proactive.

3. *Let go.* If you embrace what is being projected onto you, it will cloud your perspective and can cause you to become defensive. How do you stop this from happening? Simply tell yourself, "I'm not owning that. I'm not receiving what they are projecting." Remind yourself that they are projecting what *they* feel, think, or would do. You always have a choice to agree or disagree, even if it's only in your mind.

When it comes to projection, you can be a victim, or you can choose to be a champion. You'll find your answer in your willingness to be honest with yourself.

Remember, you may not get it right straight out of the gate. Championing yourself, self-honesty, and all the different facets we've discussed is a marathon, not a sprint.

Pull Up Your C.H.A.I.R.— Action Items

As your coach, I encourage you to take these actions:

- Starting today, commit to being aware when you are projecting onto others.

- Starting today, commit to being aware when others are projecting onto you.

- Keep track of these scenarios and situations in your self-reflection journal.

- Now make a decision as to how you will respond and deal with self-honesty, self-deception, and projection in the future.

"A"—
ADAPTABILITY

A note to my readers:

Being adaptable has never been more important than it is today ... in your career and your life! Adaptability is your capacity to accommodate and adjust to changes in your environment. You cannot afford to be the person who says, "This can't be happening!" or "We've always done it this way." You cannot hide from change, and you cannot stay with what has "always been." You have to be the person who is open to new ideas, new ways of doing things, and charting your own course.

> **Being adaptable has never been more important than it is today.**

As you read this section, consider how you will do the following:

- Adapt to changes in your responsibilities, due to new management

- Adapt to shifts in work priorities to meet a need caused by a change in expectations

- Adapt to new strategies on how to improve and/or monitor your workload, or that of your team

- Adapt to changes in job titles, job descriptions, and new work processes that entail a new way of operating

- Adapt to unforeseen events in your life

The one constant in the world is change! And your adaptability will go a long way to determine how far you will advance in your career.

CHAPTER

1

THE ART OF THE SHIFT-ABILITY

BEING FLEXIBLE AND AGILE

*Change is the only constant in life. One's ability to adapt
to those changes will determine your success in life.*
—BENJAMIN FRANKLIN

When I moved to Washington, DC, I learned a lesson that also applies to many small businesses and global corporations: your to-do list is usually blown up by ten o'clock in the morning. In the DC area, and especially in politics, things change and happen so quickly that you do not get a lot of notice.

In stark contrast to this, I've also worked with people in business and political organizations who will absolutely shut down if something comes up that they didn't plan for that day. Or if they're given a new project and someone says, "Can you get this done by such and such a time?" these same people will fall apart.

The higher up you go on the corporate ladder, the more adaptable you need to be.

If you are serious about leadership, or your desire to be in a leadership role, you have to be *adaptable*. You have to be flexible, and you have to be agile. You have to know how—and when—to shift your attention, to reprioritize your to-do list, to change your team's direction, or whatever else is needed to adapt to the next change coming your way. If you don't, you will be left behind.

Whether you are leading yourself or leading others, adaptability will win you favor, a promotion, or a raise as quickly as anything else you can do.

Here's a truth to remember: the higher up you go on the corporate ladder, the more adaptable you need to be—to business demands, to schedules, and to people.

For instance, when I moved into my role as an executive vice president in the restaurant industry, I learned quickly that my schedule wasn't really mine. I would start my day by going over my schedule that my assistant had set for the day and reviewing my to-do list so I knew what direction to take. However, I had a boss who would randomly call me multiple times a day or show up unannounced in my office. It did not matter if I had one-on-ones with my team, a meeting on Capitol Hill, or a call with the White House. When my boss said, "I need to see you, and I need to see you right now," guess what I did? I adapted my agenda to incorporate her needs.

Not only did I want to make my boss happy, but I also wanted to teach my team what it meant to be flexible and adaptable. I had to model what I wanted them to know. I coached them by saying, "You may have four or five things on your list that day, but if a new deadline comes up, or a new project, or if something happens that is unexpected, then your to-do list is no longer *the* to-do list." I had to model this behavior and exactly what I wanted my team to learn.

I want to pause here for a moment and address something that might be going through your head.

> You may be drawing a parallel between "course correcting" in chapter 6 and being flexible and adaptable in this section. Here is the connection: course correcting is *what you do*, and being flexible and adaptable is *how* you do it.

Having said this, I have also been the person interrupting someone else's schedule, and I've had so many people get flustered with me. I mean literally, visibly, emotionally triggered when I would say, "Stop what you're doing and come with me," or "I'll give you five minutes and then meet me at the elevator. We're going to the Hill, and here's what we are going to do."

As you continue to read, ask yourself, "Am I adaptable? Am I flexible? Do I get visibly flustered when change occurs?" Be honest with yourself. If you said yes to the last question, then it's time for you to figure out whatever it is that's driving your inflexibility.

The Meaning of Being Adaptable

Simply put, adaptability is the ability to quickly respond and adjust to changing trends, innovation, destabilization, and industry shifts. It is the ability to adjust or shift without notice. It's no surprise that, in a constantly changing world, data shows adaptability is a core asset in leadership. It is also at the heart of innovation.

In their book *The Platinum Rule*, authors Tony Alessandra and Michael O'Connor note that adaptability has two distinct components: flexibility and versatility. Flexibility relates to your attitude—How willing are you to change? Versatility equates to ability—Are you truly capable of change?[8] This two-part definition of adaptability shows us that it is something we have control over.

For example, you are neck deep in a project that your boss told you needs to be completed today. Then your boss comes up to you and says, "Stop what you're doing; I have something I need your input on." Do you get flustered and fume in your mind as you follow your boss (inflexibility)? Drop what you're doing and follow along like a puppy (compliance)? Or do you remind your boss of the task and deadline that they gave you, then ask if what they currently want done is more important (adaptability)?

It has been my experience that adaptability is something that many people *think* they have but actually do not. You think that adaptability is succumbing to every whim or will from others that comes your way. But that's not the case. Instead, you are willing to pivot and refocus, change when and what is needed, *when it is truly needed.* If you don't handle these types of situations well, you're never going to be successful in a leadership role. If you

---

8   Tony Alessandra and Michael J. O'Connor, *The Platinum Rule: Discover the Four Basic Business Personalities and How They Can Lead You to Success*, New York: Warner Business Books, February 1998.

want to grow in your career, being adaptable, flexible, and agile is required. You must be able to quickly respond and adjust to trends or changes in your day, to new projects that come up, or to whatever else crosses your path.

Why Adaptability Is a Core Competency

You may have heard of the term "core competency." In business, core competencies, also known as your "core qualifications," consist of a list of your qualifications for a job. If you want to succeed as a leader—leading yourself and others—it is imperative that adaptability is one of your core competencies and part of who you are.

When adaptability is a core competency, you can stay focused on your goals but can also quickly adjust how you achieve them. As an adaptable leader, who can meet new challenges as they arise without being paralyzed by sudden change, you remain comfortable with the uncertainty that leadership can bring. Even when you're not comfortable, you remain in control of yourself and what you are doing or going to do.

In a study that followed MBA students five to nineteen years after they graduated, a strength in adaptability predicted their life satisfaction, their career satisfaction, and, in fact, their career success.[9] As well, adaptability was the strongest predictor of all the emotional and social intelligence competencies.

I'll say it again: if you want to be a *successful* leader, adaptability must be one of your core competencies.

---

9   Daniel Goleman, "How Adaptability Will Define Your Career," Korn Ferry, accessed September 2021, https://www.kornferry.com/insights/this-week-in-leadership/adaptability-the-surprisingly-strong-predictor-of-career-success.

Show that you can adjust your style of working, that you can change your communication and approach to match changing situations, tasks, coworkers/people, teams, and work demands. Demonstrate that you can adjust to meet new deadlines. Show that you can adapt your activities and attitude in order to work as effectively as possible in new work environments. Be willing to try new approaches to changing situations. Stay positive. When situations change, embrace them with a positive mindset—even if this goes against what you feel inside.

> **When situations change, embrace them with a positive mindset—even if this goes against what you feel inside.**

The Benefits of Being Adaptable

How do you know if you are a person who is adaptable? If you really want to know the answer, then ask—ask your team, your management, your family. And be willing to hear what they have to say; after all, you have already learned that self-honesty is a key to being your own best champion.

There are some excellent personal benefits to being flexible. Here are just a few:

1. *You become more valuable.* The ability of an organization to adapt has been called the new competitive advantage. The same is true for individuals: employers increasingly want workers who can adapt to an ever-changing workplace. Your boss, employer, or organization will always value adaptability. Your ability to anticipate change and remain calm when things don't go as planned will give you a competitive edge in your current and future roles.

2. *You become a better leader.* Adaptable people earn respect from their peers and management. Your ability to be flexible will inspire others to be the same way, because you're setting the example. Adaptability is the "grease" that keeps a project moving or keeps a meeting in a productive mode.

3. *You achieve personal satisfaction.* Being adaptable will keep you in a positive mindset and help you see any change that comes your way as a positive challenge, and a way for you to grow your skill set. When you face a challenge and figure out a way to overcome, you'll feel more confident in yourself, which leads to personal satisfaction. You can tell yourself that you have the skills and ability needed, and champion yourself in the moment.

4. *You can better handle career transitions.* More than ever, today's political and business climate is in constant flux. What if a job or position opens up that you weren't planning for, but that you've always desired? You can complain about this being the wrong time, or you can adapt with a proactive mindset and realize this is the opportunity you have been waiting for.

5. *You can more easily bounce back.* We all go through tough times; some are our own doing, and others are simply part of life. Being adaptable will help you take in stride any adversity that comes your way. Sure, you will feel down for a while. But you won't stay down. Adaptability will help you overcome any feelings of hopelessness or helplessness, and you'll say to yourself, "Okay, such and such has happened. What do I want to do? What are my next steps?"

There's a Chinese proverb that says, "The wise adapt themselves to circumstances, as water molds itself to the pitcher." I think this succinctly sums up the importance of being adaptable.

I will close with giving you my definition of leadership: being able to handle those shifts and the ability to shift without notice. In other words, leadership = adaptability.

Pull Up Your C.H.A.I.R.— Action Items

As your coach, I encourage you to take these actions:

- Think about a time when you were adaptable. What was the outcome?

- Think about a time when you were not adaptable. What was the outcome?

- How can you begin to "separate" yourself from others, so you don't project yourself onto them?

- What feelings and red flags pop up when your schedule or to-do list gets blown up?

- Practice the "maintaining your cool" strategies, so that you are prepared to handle the unexpected.

CHAPTER

8

EMBRACE THE UNKNOWN

HOW TO BE ADAPTABLE

Life isn't about waiting for the storm to pass; it's
about learning how to dance in the rain.
—VIVIAN GREENE

I had to practice embracing the unknown recently, while coaching a gentleman who told me bluntly, "I don't like Zoom. I don't like meeting with people on Zoom, and I don't like meetings on Zoom."

I asked him, "Would you like to have a traditional conference call? Or do you want to do it by email or text?"

He said again, "I don't like Zoom. I don't think I show up well."

It wasn't my place to tell him what he liked or didn't like, or whether or not he "showed up well." Instead, I said, "You know what? I totally get it. Not a problem." Sensing this was more about a fear he felt, I then said, "Let's talk about how to work on Zoom. Let's talk about how to get you more comfortable with how it works and see if I can help you move forward." My goal was to help him move past whatever fear was holding him hostage, and to help him get more comfortable in our new virtual world of business. In short, I wanted to help him become adaptable.

An "Adaptability" Game Face

A couple of years ago, I coached someone who clearly did not like what I was saying. He got visibly and emotionally triggered during the conversation. At one point I told him, "Look, when you're in situations like we're discussing, you've got to have your game face on. It doesn't matter how 'off' you feel or how triggered you are. It doesn't matter what comes up in your day that you weren't anticipating, like the new deadlines, new projects, or new job responsibilities. You've got to take a deep breath and adapt to the situation in front of you. If you truly want to be an effective leader, you've got to have a really good game face, because adaptability is so crucial to leading."

If people know you're not adaptable and they don't think you can change, I'm here to tell you that your situation *has* changed—and not for your good.

People will not want you at the table with them. When you're in those decision-making conversations, the topics and strategies change rapidly. You're dialoguing in the moment, and the team is trying to figure out a project, a goal, a strategy. If you can't go with the conversation and be adaptable in the moment, then you are not being flexible or agile when it comes to change. Maybe you had your plan laid out for what you wanted to say in the conversation ahead of time. You may not get to it, because the conversation will go a completely different way, and you have to adjust.

> **Change is a part of life. Your response is key to your success.**

I once read a Dolly Parton quote: "You can't adjust the wind, but you can adjust the sails." Those are important words to remember. Change is going to happen, whether we like it or not, whether you want it to or not. Change is a part of life. Your response is key to your success.

I hear it from hiring managers and recruiters all the time: adaptability, adaptability. It has been a topic when I've interviewed for a position and continues to be core competency that I look for in those I interview, and I ask questions to test their adaptability. I've also stressed flexibility and agility to every team I have managed.

If you are wondering what I mean by "having an adaptable game face," I mean you must maintain your cool at all times. In high-stress situations, if you allow your emotions to get the better of you, you will become blind to what is going on around you, and you won't be able to hear what others are saying.

So how do you handle stressful situations?

First, when you interpret a situation as stressful, your body equates high stress to a personal attack and goes into fight-or-flight mode. Your heart rate goes up, your breathing becomes shallow, and your mind doesn't focus on what is *actually* happening but what it *thinks* is happening—an imminent confrontation. When this happens, remind yourself that your internal reaction is normal, but you are not under attack. Accept that what you are feeling is natural.

Next, take a deep breath. Slow down your breathing—breathe deeper and exhale slower. This will flood your body with oxygen, which will help to clear your mind. While doing this, remind yourself that you've faced high stress before, you got through it, and you will get through your current situation.

Taking these steps will help you remain objective, and maintaining objectivity is key to being adaptable. You'll be able to commit to the task at hand. You'll be able to respond appropriately, while remaining flexible and agile in the moment.

Throughout your week, and in the coming weeks, take a few moments to practice what you have read. When this information becomes ingrained in you, you'll be able to implement what you are learning during times of high stress and remain adaptable as you maintain your cool.

Red Flags

I'm sure you are constantly dealing with situations that change and opportunities to assess your adaptability that arise every day.

For example, you have your day scheduled, when something comes up that completely upends your timeline. You are in the middle of a task and get interrupted by an emergency or urgent situation. Perhaps you are assigned a new task or a new deadline that you were not expecting.

Just as you are presented with opportunities to test your adaptability, you might have some red flags indicating you are not as adaptable as you think. When you get interrupted during the day, do you get flustered? When you are given new deadlines, do you feel like giving up? When your day doesn't go the way you planned, perhaps because of an urgent situation or a fire drill, how do you handle those situations? A key red flag is to recognize how you *feel* when someone or something changes your schedule or your to-do list. Being aware of how you feel will help you determine what you want to do in response to the new situation. You are *not* at the mercy of your feelings; you can choose adaptability and flexibility, despite what you feel.

In your self-reflection journal, write out how you assess your adaptability. Perhaps you are like my coaching client who didn't want to adjust to Zoom. Maybe being adaptable isn't your strong suit. If that is the case, it's time to get honest with yourself by digging deep into what really stops you from being adaptable. While I understand that some temperaments lend themselves to being more rigid, anyone and everyone can choose to be more adaptable, more flexible. The it's-my-way-or-the-highway mentality no longer rules.

Understand that adaptability is a core competency, especially in leadership, and throughout your career and professional journey. Being adaptable, quite frankly, is key to your success.

Now I want you to ask yourself, "What is holding me back?"

Perhaps you don't like change. Maybe you are resistant to new ideas and shifting circumstances. Perhaps you don't juggle multiple tasks well.

Adaptability might not be easy at first, but patience and practice will get you there. If you know you are resistant, apprehensive, or emotionally triggered by unexpected events, then for your own benefit, commit that you are going to work on your ability to be more adaptable. It's always best to be proactive, rather than waiting for someone to give you an ultimatum. Adaptable people aren't afraid of change; they will make the necessary plans to handle it.

Five Common Characteristics and Questions of Highly Adaptable People

It has been my experience that learning from others is a great shortcut to enhance my own skills. Here are five characteristics I've learned from others and continue to practice on a daily basis.[10]

1. Willing to experiment

Adaptability involves being open to trying out new ideas and methods. You would never hear an adaptable person say, "We'll do it this way because that's the way we've always done it."

2. Unafraid of failure

Not every new idea will work as expected. But being able to view setbacks or failures as an opportunity to learn and grow is an essential element of adaptability.

3. Resourceful

Adaptable people are able to think creatively to find solutions.

4. Able to see the big picture

---

10   https://transformandthrive.co.uk/blog/7-adaptability-skills/; definitions summarized for space.

An awareness of the big picture and an understanding of how things connect empowers you to see beyond potential challenges to the wider goal and motivates you to find solutions.

5. Curious

A curious mind is open to investigating new opportunities and wants to understand how and why things work. A curious person says, "What if?" instead of "That's the way we've always done it."

Please review this list a couple of times. I want to challenge you by asking, "How many of these characteristics do you recognize in yourself?"

Here are five common questions to test your adaptability:

1. Think about a situation in which you were assigned new tasks. How did you adapt to this situation?

2. How do you adjust to changing situations that you have no control over?

3. Think about a time you had to do something you had never done before. How did you approach this situation? What did you learn?

4. You had to work on a task that was outside your job description. How did you handle the situation? What was the result?

5. How would you readjust your schedule when your manager asks you to prepare a report within a day? How do you make sure that my regular tasks don't fall behind schedule?

How many of these characteristics do you recognize in yourself? If you don't recognize any of these, then ask yourself, "What is holding me back?"

You don't like change? Are you resistant to new ideas and shifting circumstances? You don't juggle multiple tasks well?

Unfortunately, if you are resistant, apprehensive, or emotionally triggered by unexpected events, then commit to doing the work necessary to be more adaptable. Adaptability opens up your mind to new ideas, makes you question the status quo, and gives you the willingness to go against convention.

Adaptability also goes hand in hand with our next strategy: impact.

Here is something to think about: 91 percent of HR recruiters say that adaptability is a key trait they look for in leaders when they're recruiting new leadership. If you really want to outshine and stand out in the job market or in your current role, it is important for you to start now in improving your adaptability skills. Doing so ensures you remain marketable even in the ever-changing business atmosphere.[11]

Having the Right Attitude about Adaptability

If you recall back in chapter 2, I talked about "attitude." You may have heard the quote "Attitude is everything," and I want to pick up on this theme by stating that your attitude has everything to do with your ability to be adaptable.

Your attitude is always a choice.

Your attitude is always a choice; it is something you decide to have or not have—negative or positive. Your attitude will determine how adaptable you will be.

---

11   The Society for Human Resource Management, "The New Talent Landscape: Recruiting Difficulty and Skills Shortages," June 2016, https://www.shrm.org/hr-today/trends-and-forecasting/research-and-surveys/documents/shrm%20new%20talent%20landscape%20recruiting%20difficulty%20skills.pdf.

As a leader, your success in leading will largely depend on your adaptability. As I'm sure you have realized by now, adaptability entails being open to new ideas and concepts. It means embracing the unknown. Adaptable leaders earn the respect of their colleagues and motivate those they lead to embrace change, making business operations and decisions as smooth as possible.

Every organization needs adaptive leadership. To be adaptive, check out these eight "be-attitudes" that will increase your adaptability, from Steve VerBurg, president of Dale Carnegie of Orange County:[12]

1. Be adventurous and try something new each day.

2. Be an initiator of change practicing constructive dissatisfaction.

3. Be flexible and embrace change with positive thoughts.

4. Be a visionary who looks at the big picture.

5. Be a strong communicator.

6. Be open to advice and support.

7. Be a person who celebrates victories.

8. Be diligent with a healthy lifestyle.

Do any or all of these resonate with you? I challenge you to commit to implementing one or more of these "be-attitudes," and practice being adaptable by staying open to changes that will certainly test your flexibility and agility.

---

12 Steve VerBurg, "8 'Be-Attitudes' to Embrace Change and Increase Adaptability," Dale Carnegie, accessed September 2021, https://ocdalecarnegie. com/8-be-attitudes-to-embrace-change-and-increase-adaptability/.

Pull Up Your C.H.A.I.R.— Action Items

As your coach, I want to challenge you with five common questions to test your adaptability:

1. Think about a situation in which you were assigned new tasks. How did you adapt to this situation?

2. How do you adjust to changing situations that you have no control over?

3. Think about a time you had to do something you had never done before. How did you approach this situation? What did you learn?

4. You had to work on a task that was outside your job description. How did you handle the situation? What was the result?

5. How would you readjust your schedule when your manager asks you to prepare a report within a day? How do you make sure that my regular tasks don't fall behind schedule?

CHAPTER

9

GET YOUR
GAME FACE ON

THE ROAD AHEAD

*Today I will do what others won't, so tomorrow
I can accomplish what others can't.*
—JERRY RICE

At the 2016 Rio Olympics, Michael Phelps was caught on camera glaring while preparing for the men's two-hundred-meter butterfly final. His look, now popularly known as "Phelps Face," is a great example of a term that most people recognize: game face.

When you hear the term "game face," you may have your own sports analogy that comes to mind. But it is also cross-industry terminology. Whether you're in business, politics, sports, or an academic environment, when you have your game face on, you are ready; you are prepared for what comes your way, and you are prepared to win.

I like this definition of "game face" found in the Cambridge dictionary: "a serious or determined expression that you put on when you are going to try to win or achieve something."

"Game face" also refers to how we mask our emotions. For example, Pete put his game face on as soon as I started to point out his responsibilities, so I can't really tell how he took the news I told him.

Having your game face on does not mean you become emotionless—that would be impossible. It means that unexpected events may emotionally trigger you, but you rise above your emotions and don't allow them to control your reactions or behavior. When a problem arises, you don't dwell on how difficult it is. Instead, you shift and adjust to find solutions. If you are working on a project and a change comes at you out of left field, you take a deep breath, stay focused, and refine your strategy to account for the unexpected.

When you have your game face on, you are ready.

Maintaining a game face that allows you to be adaptable is what effective leadership—and self-leadership—looks like in any industry. Pivot. Adapt. Rise above emotion. Stay objective. Don't take things personally. Maintaining your game face is an emotional tool that will help you stay focused on what matters most.

People with their game face on are flexible and are more likely to stay calm under pressure, while working their way through dynamic work environments. There is no it's-my-way-or-the-highway attitude, because the highway always leads to an emotional blowup.

Whether adaptability is one of your core skills or you easily get flustered and are emotionally triggered by unexpected events, you always need your game face on. All day. Every day.

Change happens.

Surprises happen.

Unexpected events occur.

And yes, we all get annoyed at times.

But you can't allow that annoyance or frustration to get the better of you. In fact, you can't get flustered. Period. Negative emotional reactions show that you are not being adaptable and can undermine your self-leadership and your leadership of others.

I know a guy who tends to be adaptable and, most of the time, has his game face on. But every once in a while, he blows up. When I asked him why, he said, "I try my best to flex, to be adaptable, to see the other person's point of view, or find a way to pivot when I'm put in a difficult position. But when I feel I've done everything I can, and nothing seems to work, or if I'm put in a corner with no way out, I come out like a roaring lion. I'm working on telling myself that there is always a way around the situation I'm in; I just have to find it or ask for help. That's how I'm working to keep my game face on all the time."

Here's another example. When I began my role leading the restaurant industry public affairs efforts, board members told me I didn't belong in that role. I was in over my head. I didn't know what I was doing. And they didn't know why I was chosen for that role. In the wake of their public comments and criticisms—yes, they publicly voiced their opinions—I had a choice to make: I could put on my game face every day, try to ignore my doubters and naysayers, and prove them wrong. Or I could succumb to what they were saying and let my emotions get the better of me. You guessed it—I put, and kept, my game face on. (I want to add that every success my team and I accomplished gave me a quiet satisfaction that I was proving them wrong.)

In November 2019, the University of Tennessee released the results of a study titled "Get Your Game Face On: Study Finds It May Help."[13]

"Game face may not only improve performance in cognitive tasks, but it could also lead to better recovery from stress," said Matthew Richesin, master's student and lead author of the study, which was coauthored with Associate Professor of Psychology Debora Baldwin, Michael Oliver, a postdoctoral fellow in the UT Graduate School of Medicine, and fellow graduate student Lahai Wicks.

When you have your game face on, you can feel an intense energy about yourself that shows you are completely in the zone. You are focused, determined, and committed to your passion and purpose. Your internal mindset and external actions are in alignment when pursing your goal.

---

13   University of Tennessee, Knoxville, "Get Your Game Face On: Study Finds It May Help," November 13, 2019, https://news.utk.edu/2019/11/13/get-your-game-face-on-study-finds-it-may-help/.

Game Face and Emotional Intelligence

In today's business and political climates, emotional intelligence, or EI, has become a hot topic. And to my way of thinking, EI is key to maintaining your game face.

Your emotional intelligence is your ability to understand and manage your own emotions. Doing so will also help those around you manage theirs. Someone with a high degree of emotional intelligence is aware of what they are feeling, what their emotions are telling them, and how their emotions affect other people.

If you want to champion yourself, if you want to succeed and accomplish all you've set out to do as a leader, then your EI is vital to your success and vital to maintaining your game face. After all, who is more likely to succeed—a leader who spews out their emotions anytime something doesn't go their way, or a leader who has their game face on, can stay in control, and can calmly assess whenever adversity comes their way?

According to Daniel Goleman, an American psychologist sometimes referred to as the founder of emotional intelligence, there are five key elements:[14]

1. Self-awareness

2. Self-regulation

3. Motivation

4. Empathy

5. Social skills

---

14   The Importance of Emotional Intelligence, "The 5 Components," accessed September 2021, http://theimportanceofemotionalintelligence.weebly.com/the-5-components.html.

If you want to be a leader who is respected, and one who can keep their game face on, then it is crucial you learn to manage yourself in these areas. Your EI will go a long way to determine your courage as a leader when you're under pressure.

> **It is better to exhibit grace under fire than to act like a victim of circumstances.**

It's human to feel disappointment, to feel frustration, to feel misunderstood. But if you pout, blow up, go into hiding, or act defensive, the simple truth is you cannot be an effective leader—and you certainly aren't championing yourself.

If you've been dealt a bad deal, admit it. If you've been thrown more challenges than there are hours in the day, own it. But before you lose your cool, go somewhere private, feel whatever emotions are rising up in you, remind yourself of what you are trying to accomplish, then get your game face on and remember that it is better to exhibit grace under fire than to act like a victim of circumstances.

Leaders who work on their ability to stay cool under pressure will always have their game face ready to wear.

It is important to address your ability to be adaptable and why your game face is a critical element of self-leadership. You can do this by coaching yourself. Here are some things to consider as you "self-coach."

What you think about yourself—what you truly believe to be true about yourself—will determine your assessment of yourself in any given situation. For example, if you are harsh and critical of yourself, you will never be happy with any outcome; you'll always feel you could have done better. If you have a kind and graceful belief about yourself, you will show up in positive and energetic ways.

Why is this true?

Your actions follow your thoughts.

There have been times when I've lost my cool, felt overstressed, and reacted in ways I regretted. I have also learned that to lead myself, and to be successful, I must choose my thoughts *wisely* and *deliberately*.

Whenever you find yourself overstressed or feeling anxious in a negative situation, it is vitally important that you coach yourself during these times. How do you do this? When your attitude is unproductive, tell yourself to shift from negative thought patterns to productive ones. You have to deliberately choose the positive over the negative. Change the fearful thoughts to *I can do this*. Remind yourself of your conviction and have faith in your skills and talents. Focus on your ability to meet your challenges and your goals.

Learn to coach yourself into a positive state of mind that will produce productivity. Doing so will lead to positive momentum and forward movement that can be revitalized whenever you're facing a potential setback.

Think of your attitude with this equation: energy = motion. From this paradigm, attitude determines movement forward or backward.

As this chapter comes to a close, let me ask you this: Are you serious about leading yourself and others? Truly serious? Are you willing to do what you need to do to step up and step out? If so, then you must get your game face on. Every. Single. Day.

Pull Up Your C.H.A.I.R.— Action Items

As your coach, I want to challenge you to consider the following:

1. What are you really like and how do you react when you're under pressure?

2. How and when do you get your game face on?

3. What situations cause you to take your game face off?

4. In your self-reflection journal, write down the five key elements of emotional intelligence, study these, and determine who you can apply them to in your life.

"I"—IMPACT

A note to my readers:

We have journeyed together through these strategies to the point where I can share my ultimate secret ingredient: impact. What you are about to read in this chapter is not someone else's theory. It's my hidden skill and secret weapon.

Think about impact in this way: championing yourself gets you to the table. Impact ensures you stay there.

Impact is a catalyst for change, and a foundational strategy to your career and leadership success.

What I'm going to discuss in this chapter has accelerated and propelled my career to a level of success I used to dream about. The views

> **Championing yourself gets you to the table. Impact ensures you stay there.**

and insights I share about "impact" are mine and mine alone, based on twenty-five years of experience.

I have intentionally sought to be a person of impact to advance my growth trajectory, so get ready to open your mind to a new way of thinking.

As you read this section, remember this: you were born to make an impact … so make it good.

CHAPTER

10

CHANGE THE OUTCOME

WHY IMPACT IS CRUCIAL
TO YOUR SUCCESS

The only limit to your impact is your imagination and commitment.
—TONY ROBBINS

So far, I have given you four personal, specific examples of how I championed my value during an interview, how I championed myself when starting a new job, how I championed myself when asking for a promotion, and how I championed myself when I applied for a new job at a new organization. I'm sure you can see there is an obvious pattern here. I articulated my value and my contributions and what I had to offer in each example. These are directly connected to having an *impact*.

I learned the importance of impact by accident.

In 2008, US senator Barack Obama was running against fellow US senator John McCain to be president of the United States. I began my tenure for Dunkin' only a few months before the presidential nominees of both parties were named. One day, I was copied on an email about a new marketing campaign being contemplated for Baskin-Robbins. (Dunkin' Brands is the franchisor and corporate parent of Dunkin' Donuts and Baskin-Robbins.)

The email described two new flavors of ice cream: a chocolate/vanilla swirl for Democratic nominee Barack Obama, and a peanut brittle for Republican nominee John McCain. These new flavors were ready for launch.

When I read the email, my immediate response was "Oh no!" I immediately began to panic … Was I the only one who sees the problem here?

Barack Obama is biracial, and there was no way the brand could do a chocolate/vanilla swirl ice cream for Mr. Obama! And John McCain, the revered war hero, was seventy-one and facing questions about his age and health. Was I the only one who saw a major PR problem with a peanut brittle ice cream for an older candidate?

I didn't know what to do. Do I respond? Should I not respond? Are people going to get mad if I point out how offensive these flavors may be to our customers? Will I get in trouble from my boss?

Seriously, I did not know what to do. I was the new kid on the block and was going to point out an obvious flaw in the brand marketing strategy. Who was I do to that?

To this day, I don't know who thought to bring me into the conversation, but I was so glad they did. I was the political person, and if I didn't say anything and this blew up, would I be asked, "Why didn't you say anything?" I weighed the pros and cons and decided to respond to the group with my concerns.

I typed out my trepidations, but I also offered solutions, including another way to celebrate and honor the historic nature of the 2008 election. I held my breath and hit send.

Are you wondering what happened?

A few minutes later, I saw email responses hit my in-box. I took a deep breath and opened each one.

The responses were unanimous! They thanked me for my concerns *and* for offering an alternative approach that still accomplished their stated goals.

Now, don't get me wrong. I've had a tremendous impact when working for two congressmen. It is hard not to have an impact when you are leading a congressman's legislative agenda and advising him on votes and all legislative matters in the House of Representatives.

But this was different.

I was the new employee dealing with senior officials in the company. I was confident in my assessment of the marketing campaign but did not know if others would share my point of view. I pointed out my concerns but also helped them "get to yes" by taking a different approach to reach their stated goals and objectives.

The team's positive response to my approach was overwhelming! And that is when I realized the power of having an impact by helping people "get to yes."

I'll explain what "get to yes" means shortly, but I assure you that you can help people do the same.

Impact and championing yourself through self-leadership and leading others go hand in hand. When you have an impact, you are in essence championing yourself—you're "raising your hand" in different ways and offering a different approach or solution to accomplish stated goals.

I encourage you from this moment forward to look for ways to make an impact in your environment. Whenever you are in a meeting, look for roadblocks that come up while discussing solutions, listen to the naysayers and their reasons, and note those who have "analysis paralysis" or those who are stymied by the situation. Once you've identified the negative, start thinking of ways over, around, or through the obstacles. You may be able to do this in the spur of the moment, or you may need some time to think this through. Either way, be willing to say something like, "I know this is an issue, and I'd like to offer a few thoughts to consider." Then calmly and politely state your thoughts. When others start to see aha moments, including new possibilities and solutions, you will be making an impact by getting them to yes … and impact is crucial to your success.

Impact versus Influence

I chose the word "impact" instead of "influence" for this section for one main reason: influence is a loaded word, similar to "confidence" in the chapter on championing yourself. People subscribe their own theories to the definition of influence and their own level of influence.

However, impact is a "visual" word; when you hear or visualize the word "impact," it creates a picture in your mind of something powerful. Second, impact is something you *feel* in your body; the word creates a sensation within you.

A person of impact doesn't just have influence. Influence is *having the capacity* to have an effect on character, decision-making, behavior, etc. Impact *is* the effect—not just the capability to have an effect. If you're aiming to influence someone, influence a meeting, or influence a decision, then you are selling yourself short. Influence can be misperceived and even misinterpreted, whereas having an impact is hard hitting and a game changer. Impact gets to the point of what you're trying to do.

> **Influence is *having the capacity* to have an effect; impact *is* the effect.**

As a leader, or someone striving to be in a leadership role, your goal is to have an impact every single day. Influence wanes and can diminish. Impact is lasting and irreplaceable.

When you have an impact, you are literally speaking up to change an outcome, a direction, a decision, or a goal. That's why I call impact "influence plus"! Impact is influence on steroids. Impact means you are forward thinking, you are forward leaning. You are getting things done in ways that create dynamic change.

Some of the stories and examples I've previously shared illustrate how I've championed myself to get me to the table with the decision makers. But remember this: championing yourself gets you *to* the table, and impact *keeps* you there.

How to Get to Yes

In my Baskin-Robbins story in the above section, my panic and trepidation arose from the fact that it is easy to share concerns and pitfalls about someone else's approach and strategy. It is much harder to offer a solution that still accomplishes the stated goals while offering an alternative path to accomplish those goals. It is why the single best way to have an impact and to differentiate yourself is to help others "get to yes."

I'm sure you're asking, "What do you mean by helping people 'get to yes'?" The phrase means helping your audience see past whatever limitations are in front of them, then offering ways, views, direction, etc. that will help them see possibilities and solutions. Your audience may be a board of directors, a CEO, a leadership team, or your own team. In my case, my audience can also include coaching clients and lobbying clients.

Here are a couple of illustrations:

- You are reading emails going back and forth among your team, and you realize they are missing something in their conversation. Do you say something that will bring about clarification and move the team toward yes?

- You are in an in-person or Zoom team meeting, listening to the conversation and thinking, *I have something to say that will affect the outcome.* Do you speak up and offer a different perspective?

If you want to help others to "get to yes"—and make an impact—then you are obligated to say something or do something. You have to risk being told that you are wrong (even if you know you're right) or being told to keep your views and opinions to yourself.

To be clear, your own goals and agendas are different than helping people "get to yes." The latter means you are focused on the other person(s). You are hearing their goals and agendas. So your mindset, your outlook, and the path you take are going to be different … and that's how you have an impact.

It is easy to sit in meetings or in a group and join the naysayers, the excuse makers. It is easy to say why something can't be done. It is much harder to say, "Yes, it can be done, and here is how you can accomplish your objectives."

Others will notice and remember. I promise.

Throughout my career, I've made a practice of being a "What if?" person and helping others "get to yes." I was willing to explain why X or Y would be worth exploring or worth consideration. Do you know where this got me? People started inviting me to meetings, even if I wasn't directly on their team. I would also be invited to executive and board meetings to offer my perspective and points of view. I wasn't afraid to insert myself into the conversation or into a project. I didn't have a self-promotion agenda; I simply wanted to help accomplish the desired outcome.

In my current role as CEO and founder of Summit Public Affairs, companies hire me to help them "get to yes." They have a goal to achieve in Washington—with Congress, the president, and/or the administration. They tell me the goal, and it is my job to offer a how-to-get-to-yes strategy and solution.

That's how you lead others to yes, and that's how you become a person of impact.

I Don't Believe in Impostor Syndrome

I don't believe in impostor syndrome. I truly don't. I know there are books, courses, speeches, and various kinds of materials about how to deal with impostor syndrome. I also understand that it is easy to give in to the idea that you are an impostor.

Here is why I do not believe in it.

Impostor syndrome is a belief that you are not as competent as others perceive you to be, even if you have the skill set.

Impostor syndrome is built on what is called a "limiting belief" you have about yourself. Limiting beliefs are the negative thoughts and opinions about ourselves that we believe are the absolute truth. These beliefs stop us from moving forward in our lives, from accomplishing our personal and professional goals.

Impostor syndrome means that you are questioning your value, contributions, skills, and talents. As we discussed in the section on championing yourself, we don't doubt our value, contribution, skills, and talents. Instead, we tout and leverage our skills, talents, value, accomplishments, and contributions to our advantage.

When you do the work, you are not an impostor. You know your skills, talents, and the value you offer. You have worked so hard to reach the position you are in, and maybe you have higher aspirations. Why would you undermine yourself by thinking you are an impostor? That you don't belong at the decision-making table? I assure you, when you have done the hard work to get to the table, you are not an impostor. However, you have to believe that you *belong* at that table—nobody is going to do that for you.

You are not an impostor. You a person of impact.

Keep in mind that when I started in Congress, I had no congressional or legislative experience. When I started at Dunkin', I did not have restaurant industry or business experience. If there were ever times when I could have felt like an impostor, those two career moves would be at the top of my list.

But I was never an impostor. Why? Because I did the work.

When I started my career in Congress, a chief of staff to another member befriended me. I confided in him that I didn't have congressional or legislative experience. He took me to lunch and explained how to be a legislative director. I took his advice and excelled in that role for two congressmen, one a freshman member and the other a senior member. Two very different legislative models with different opportunities and challenges, and I mastered both.

When I started at Dunkin', I would sit in company and industry meetings and take pages and pages of notes. Then I went home at night and studied the notes on my legal pad. I was determined to work hard to learn the information I did not know.

Legendary basketball coach Pat Summitt said it best: "Here's how I am going to beat you. I'm going to outwork you. That's it. That's all there is to it."

To echo Coach Summitt's words, "That's all there is to it."

To be the best at what you do, you have to be willing to work harder than everyone else. What I mean by "work harder" is that you do your homework; you put in the hours; you get the necessary training and education; you learn from others. You do what needs to be done to get where you want to go. And when you work harder and strive to be the best you can be, you are not an impostor.

You can choose to be a victim of your past, or you can choose to be the pilot of your own destiny.

My parents instilled in me the lessons of hard work. If I wanted to be the best, I needed to work harder than everyone else and do the work no one else wanted to do.

Perhaps you didn't have parents like mine. Maybe there wasn't anyone in your younger years who encouraged you to do your best. That's no excuse not to step out and step up, and to do what needs to be done. Whether or not you had good role models, you should be—in fact, you have to be—the role model you want in your life.

You can choose to be a victim of your past, or you can choose to be the pilot of your own destiny.

When you reflect upon the hard work do you every day, day in and day out, and see the difference you have made in your role, your team, and your organization, there is no logical reason for you to feel like an impostor. If a limiting belief is telling you differently, then you must challenge what it says.

Limiting beliefs are thoughts and opinions that you believe to be the absolute truth—even if they are not true. They have a negative impact on your life by stopping you from moving forward and growing on a personal and professional level. I would even go as far as to say that limiting beliefs are the number one reason for your not accomplishing your goals.

To test this out, the next time you are in a meeting and want to say something but don't, ask yourself, "Why didn't I speak up?" Then think about how you were feeling in that moment. You can then trace your feelings back to your thoughts about yourself. The question then becomes, "Why were you thinking those thoughts?" Once you identify the reason, you will have identified the limiting belief. And once the limiting belief has been exposed, you can choose whether or not you want that belief to continue to control what you do or don't do.

Do you *feel* like you are not doing a good job? Then examine the facts of your work. Do you *feel* like you can't make a difference? Then remind yourself of all the times you have made a difference.

When impostor syndrome creeps up, tell yourself *out loud*, "I am not an impostor. I belong here. I deserve to be here. I will not doubt my self-worth, my worth to others, or my competency." Say this as many times as you need to, for as long as you need to.

Why do I say to tell yourself these things out loud? There is a psychological principle that when we hear the voice of someone else, our mind says there is a fifty-fifty chance that what they are saying is true. However, when we hear our own voice, our mind says that our words must be true.

I want to be clear that doubting is not the same as impostor syndrome. When you doubt, you are really questioning. When you are an impostor, you feel like a fraud, even if you are wearing a positive facade.

Do I doubt myself at times? Sure.

But do I feel like an impostor? Absolutely not!

Remember the sage advice the congressman gave me back in chapter 2? When you view yourself as an equal, you will be viewed as an equal.

I encourage you to make this a mantra and repeat this phrase to yourself: "When I view myself as an equal, I will be treated as an equal. When I view myself as an equal, I am not an impostor."

Pull Up Your C.H.A.I.R.— Action Items

As your coach, I want to challenge you to consider the following:

1. Write down what you believe is the difference between "impact" and "influence."

2. What are some ways you can start to have an impact in your sphere?

3. What are some ways you can help others "get to yes"?

4. Do you identify with the impostor syndrome? If so, what mantra can you come up with that you can repeat daily to combat it?

CHAPTER

11

ASK "WHAT IF?"

HOW TO BE A PERSON OF IMPACT

There are three types of people: those who make things happen, those who watch things happen, and those who wonder what happened.
—TOM GATHERS

In Washington, DC, during the first year of a new president, it's always hard for the administration to get things done, because they're finding their way. They're still looking for the bathrooms, their staff is still finding their seats, and everyone is trying to figure out their roles.

In my role as executive vice president and chief lobbyist for the restaurant industry, I already had experience dealing with the ever-changing political environment. However, I was hired to develop and lead a new advocacy strategy for the industry (the second-largest private sector employer in the country). When I was given the marching orders to wipe the slate clean and start anew, I knew I had to teach my team to be "What if?" people in order to accomplish the bold goals for which I was being asked to lead.

A "What if?" person challenges the status quo. "What if?" creates out-of-the-box thinking. You are helping others see new possibilities, new directions, and new outcomes.

I sat in meetings in which I shared an insight, gave my views and opinions, or made a request. And my team members often told me no, or said, "That's not how we do things here."

Seriously, my team of fifty would give me those types of answers. They did not want to hear new perspectives. It didn't matter that the board and CEO were asking us to chart a different course to produce impactful policy outcomes for the industry. Some of the team members were not interested in looking at matters a different way or dreaming of bold outcomes and results.

Now, it would have been easy to feel embarrassed or ashamed, then to shut my mouth and not say a word. Instead, I said, "Just give me a chance to help you understand (whatever we were discussing)." Again, I was told no and given every reason in the book why something wasn't going to work. It would have been easy for me to get angry and say, "Look, you are on *my* team, and you will do what

I say, or find another job!" Sometimes I had to take a hard line, but I also knew I needed to teach them these skills that would be valuable in their current role and future roles. I wanted to help them expand their views and ideas and to think out of the box.

In one meeting, I explained to my team that they could be either a "What if?" or a "No, but …" person. "What if?" people are those who acknowledge any roadblocks, but keep the end goal in mind, and offer advice and direction and present solutions that go over, around, or through any barriers. On the other hand, "No, but …" people have a that's-not-going-to-work or a this-is-the-way-we've-always-done-it mindset. The problem? Within my sphere of influence, there were way too many "No, but …" people and few who were "What if?" individuals. True to my nature as a "What if?" person, I urged them to adopt the same mindset, and if you want to be a person of impact, I urge you to do the same.

With a "What if?" mindset to create enormous impact and results, my team successfully changed the way we approached industry-related needs and concerns, and the way we would approach governmental power brokers. We did this in terms of having an *impact* versus just having an *influence*. And I'm happy to say that we had the most success affecting public policy in both political and business arenas than the restaurant industry had seen in two decades. (That's what I was told.)

If you want to have an impact, it all goes back to Congresswoman Chisholm's quote: "If they don't give you a seat at the table, bring a folding chair."

Do you want to know what gets you to the table and keeps you there? It's impact. And impact comes from being a "What if?" person. It is the impact you have on your team and other teams, and the impact you have on the organization—that's the secret sauce to being an excellent and proficient leader. Impact is also the trait of a leader who stays in a leadership role and continues to expand their role and their reach.

Having an impact guarantees lasting success.

If you want to have an impact, then you must intentionally and purposefully pull up your chair to the table and raise your hand. You've done your homework, and you are prepared. You have a voice, and you are going to use it in a respectful and impactful way. When you have an impact, you ensure success, and having an impact guarantees lasting success.

The Shift to "What If?"

My "What if?" philosophy has been with me for almost two decades. I can trace its roots back to 2008. I was working for Dunkin' and had two bosses, the CEO and the CCO, who both embraced and encouraged me to work with the senior leadership team to provide new perspectives and solutions. They knew I was a person who asked "What if?" and that my solutions were based on my experience, which was different than everyone else's in the room. I had a different point of view, a different perspective, and I could think outside the box.

In addition to coming into the company environment from a different perspective, the ultimate "What if?" exercise was offering possibilities and solutions to all our stakeholders: elected officials, their staff, internal employees, our franchisees, and our industry partners.

Here are some of the ways having a "What if?" mindset created a positive outcome.

MARKETING TO KIDS

There was an onslaught of new regulations coming out of the Obama administration about what food companies could and could not do, when marketing to kids. This was a critical issue for the restaurant industry and Baskin-Robbins in particular. (Dunkin' and Baskin-Robbins were owned by the same company.)

Under the proposed regulations, our franchises could no longer offer birthday cakes, and they could no longer offer stick figures such as GI Joe, SpongeBob SquarePants, or other frozen characters on top of an ice cream cake. These types of figures were being interpreted by the government as marketing to kids. This would greatly affect the way all small businesses advertised, including any healthy products being offered.

Since this new marketing initiative could have a huge, negative impact on Baskin-Robbins, we took a different approach with members of Congress and appealed on a philanthropic level. We asked, "What if we could no longer sponsor Little League baseball teams? What if we could no longer provide financing for the local girls' soccer team? What if we could no longer give money to local communities, because any of these scenarios could be interpreted as marketing to kids? What if we could no longer give to foundations such as Make-A-Wish or St. Jude?"

We told regulatory officials that with the government agencies targeting thirteen different types of marketing to kids, Dunkin' and Baskin-Robbins could no longer offer any type of philanthropic endeavor under the new agenda—and that would be devastating to countless organizations that depended on our support in local communities. This was something the regulators had not considered. The "What if?" strategy had a huge impact on members of Congress, as my leadership team and I looked for other ways to say, "Hey, we are really good partners for communities. We give to all kinds of charities, but all of our efforts could be interpreted as marketing to kids."

We were raising our collective hands to offer a different perspective and approach. And it worked! The marketing-to-kids regulations were abandoned.

COUNTING CALORIES

This a big one … literally!

You know the calorie counts you see on restaurant menus and menu boards? A "What if?" strategy is why consumers across the country now see that information.

The "What if?" strategy for calorie display began in 2008, when states and cities across the country began dictating to restaurants why and how they were to display calorie information. The trouble was a lack of cohesive direction. One city said the calorie font was to be size ten, while another specified size eight. One state determined that sodium intake was to be displayed, while another dictated that portions, in terms of ounces, were to be noted. For restaurants with locations across the country, this was shaping up to be a nightmare. There were twenty-two states and countless cities that had their own calorie legislation—and this was just getting started!

At that time, I was the newest lobbyist in the restaurant industry, having just left my work on Capitol Hill, working for Congressman Cooper. To my surprise, my new boss at Dunkin' told me that he wanted me to colead the restaurant coalition! He valued the political relationships I had built, and he believed I was the one who could connect best with members of Congress and the industry's regulators. I was honored and began to dedicate 50 percent of my time toward this endeavor.

After some in-depth strategizing sessions, our coalition went to Congress with a bold "What if?" strategy. We told Congress that we understood calorie intake was becoming a major issue. The trouble from our side was the patchwork of laws and regulations from state to state, county to county, and city to city. We then presented our solution: "What if Congress could create one uniform national standard that would regulate calories on menus in restaurants across the country?" As an industry, we had never asked Congress for regulation. Now we were asking for Congress to regulate us. Talk about bold! This would reduce administrative costs for individual restaurants and franchisees, and for the industry as a whole, while giving regulators and health officials the information consumers wanted. We also noted this was the right thing to do for the public at large; it would eliminate confusion among consumers and bring clarity and uniformity. Consumers deserved to have the same information from state to state and city to city.

However, this was just the start of the story.

Not until 2018—ten years later—did I see the fruit of my labor leading this initiative. From the Obama administration to the Trump administration, we continued with a single-minded pursuit to get federal legislation passed that would create a uniform calorie standard for all restaurants. This became an ultimate "What if?" because the outcome would be displayed and judged for years to come.

During these ten years, I left Dunkin' and became the executive vice president and chief lobbyist for the National Restaurant Association. It was now my job to lead this initiative to a successful conclusion on behalf of the restaurant industry. I was a Blue Dog Democrat leading a business association, so people automatically assumed I couldn't work with the Trump administration. However, I told my team that nothing could be further from the truth; we were going to have the ultimate impact by forming a new partnership with the new administration. We would accomplish our public policy goals.

We then rolled up our sleeves and went to work with the new administration, showing them why and how the restaurant industry—and the public—would suffer under the patchwork of state and city laws. We explained why having a uniform federal law for calorie display actually led to *less* regulation, something the Trump administration was focused on. We appealed to what they wanted to get done, and how a new federal law helped the administration meet their agenda. We stated why the law was needed, and that even though industries don't normally ask for regulation, there was an absolute necessity to have this oversight. We went through all the mechanisms needed to help the administration implement the regulation within the Food and Drug Administration (FDA). In the spring of 2018, the FDA enacted the final regulation, and lo and behold, I have pictures from 2018 showing my team and me celebrating our successful ten-year journey!

Today, whenever I give a speech and the topic of calories comes up, I always joke that when my audience sees calorie details on the menu, they can blame me. It is my fault. Talk about having an impact with a "What if?" strategy! This one was history in the making.

Keep in mind that all the successes in my career have been based on a "What if?" impact strategy.

Today, whether I am working with an industry or an individual, the value of this strategy holds true. When a company or industry hires me to represent them in Washington, I'm often asked how I can work in such a chaotic environment. I reply, "Where you see chaos, I see clarity. When you see chaos on TV, I see good partners whom I can work with." Do you want to work with the Department of Labor? Here is how we can accomplish that. Do you want to partner with

Congress? Here is how the "What if?" strategy can get you to the table and keep you there.

The same "What if?" strategy holds true for individuals who hire me as their coach. As with all the strategies in this book, this one is universal.

The most potent aspect of asking "What if?" is that you are never pointing fingers. You are never laying the blame on someone who might really be to blame. "What if?" opens up the mind. It opens up the heart. It opens up collaboration. It also creates a tangible impact that reverberates throughout your team or organization … and even the public at large.

Let's pause a moment so you can do some work in your self-reflection journal.

Write down the following questions:

Am I a "What if?" kind of person?

Or am I a "No, but …" person?

Am I someone who says, "We've always done it that way because that's the way it's always done"?

Or am I someone who asks, "What if? How can I think outside the box? How can I see outside the box?"

Be honest as you answer these questions.

Always remember that to be a person of impact and to reach your full potential, you must be a "What if?" kind of person.

"No, But …" versus "Yes, And …"

I'm sure you recall in the last chapter that I talked about helping people "get to yes" and in doing so you can help that person, team, or organization reach their goals.

Another way to say "What if?" is to say, "Yes, and ..." As you will see, these two phrases go hand in hand.

In essence, "Yes, and ..." means that you understand what the goal or agenda is. You are then going to help the person/team/organization reach their goals, but in a way they may not have previously considered. "Yes, and ..." means you are offering to find a solution in a way that is different from the norm. You are not changing the goal, just offering different ideas, solutions, and paths to accomplish that goal.

You don't offer excuses.

You don't say why something can't be done.

You become the "Yes, and ..." person.

You are saying, "Yes, the goal can be accomplished, and here are some new ways to consider to reach that goal."

"No, but ..." people are the excuse makers. The ones who want the easy way out and do as little work as possible. They like the status quo. Simply put, it is easy to say no. It is easy to make excuses as to why something cannot be done. Saying no is easy. Saying yes is much harder.

> **Once you have something to offer, you are not only *at* the table but you are also *setting* the table.**

Here is an example.

You are in a meeting with a team of peers and upper management. The discussion centers around how to increase revenues. You have already done your homework, and it is time for you to speak up. You say, "Yes, we can increase revenues, and here are a few observations based on my research and experience. What if ..." This is an incredibly tactful way of expanding your cross-functional and organizational reach. And this is exactly why you have to know your stuff and be confident in your abilities and capabilities.

Once you have something to offer, you are not only *at* the table but you are also *setting* the table. And setting the table means you are having an impact. I know this is true because I've been in this position, and I continue to make sure that I set the table whenever I can.

If you want to contribute to key initiatives, even though it may not be part of your job description, then leverage opportunities to say, "Yes, and ..." for impact.

Even if something isn't in your lane, but you have information you think can be valuable, you can say, "Perhaps you should think about ..." or, "Based on my experience, X may be an option."

In closing, here is something to consider. You may have heard of the "ten times your effort" principle. In his summary of the book *The 10X Rule*, by Grant Cardone, James Clear notes that:

> the 10X Rule says that 1) you should set targets for yourself that are 10X greater than what you believe you can achieve and 2) you should take actions that are 10X greater than what you believe are necessary to achieve your goals. The biggest mistake most people make in life is not setting goals high enough. Taking massive action is the only way to fulfill your true potential.[15]

I can guarantee you that the way to increase your impact times ten is by using "What if?" and "Yes, and ..." whenever and wherever possible.

---

15   James Clear, *"The 10X Rule* by Grant Cardone," JamesClear.com, accessed September 2021, https://jamesclear.com/book-summaries/10x-rule.

Pull Up Your C.H.A.I.R.— Action Items

As your coach, I want to challenge you to consider the following:

- In your journal, write out the "What if?" strategy in your own words.

- Review your answers to the questions on page 161. Is there anything you need to change?

- How can you apply the "What if?" strategy to a current or past situation?

- How can you apply the ten-times principle in your business or career?

CHAPTER

12

PREPARE FOR IMPACT

THE ROAD AHEAD

Genius is in the idea. Impact, however, comes from action!
—*SIMON SINEK*

You have done your homework, and you are ready. You feel confident and prepared. You are forward leaning, forward thinking. It's time to "raise your hand" and have the impact you want to have. And if you think about it, your impact can be staggering. Whether you are impacting a small team or a large organization, your impact can and will have a ripple effect.

I believe there are three types of impact: personal, team, and organizational.

Personal

Ultimately, your life is about you—what you want to do, how you want to do it, and when and where you want to do it. You want to have an impact and make a difference in your personal life. How do you do that?

Here are some unique ways you can impact yourself.

1. Live in today.

Regardless of your present circumstances, good or bad, live in the "now." In good times, celebrate. In trials, look to see what you need to learn in order to grow. Focusing on personal growth, instead of being fearful of whatever you are facing, will keep you moving in a forward trajectory. Living in the now doesn't mean you forget about your past or that you don't consider the future. It means that you don't allow your past to control you, but you live, learn, and grow today in ways that will impact your future.

2. Be prepared.

The truth is that preparation might be hard work, but hard work will get you where you want to go. When you've prepared, when you've done the necessary work, you will feel confident, and having confidence makes a direct impact on yourself. Here are some ways you can make sure you are prepared:

- Prep before meetings. Review out loud what you've done, which will increase your confidence.

- Get the hard tasks done in the morning. When these are completed, you eliminate the sense of dread that often accompanies hard tasks.

- Prioritize short- and long-term tasks. Know what you need to do, when you need to do it.

3. Celebrate.

One of the best ways you can impact yourself and others is by celebrating the small wins as well as the big triumphs. Just because you have yet to achieve a major goal or milestone, that doesn't mean you can't enjoy where you are today. Celebrate big wins. Celebrate small wins.

4. Rest.

You can be driven to accomplish goals, to make an impact. But you can also drive yourself over a cliff, and crash and burn. If you don't take time to rest, relax, and enjoy life, you are heading for burnout sooner or later. Trust me on this: I've been one of those hard-driving professionals whose health suffered from stress and lack of sleep. No matter what you are doing, no matter what deadline you are facing, even if you do something as simple as taking a walk around the block, you must prioritize your health. Remember, sleep and relaxation pay lifetime dividends.

Team

Impacting your team means you take your eyes off yourself and do what is best for those around you. You may have heard the saying, "There is no 'I' in team." The best way to impact your team is to have an others-first attitude.

Inc.com notes there are three things people notice that can help or hinder the impact you have on your team: your attitude, how you treat others, and how you act when you think no one is watching.[16]

Here are some ways you can have a positive impact on your team:

1. *Build trust.* I'll say this succinctly: no trust, no relationship equals no team. Building trust is easy if you continually practice being a person of your word. Whenever possible, do what you say, and say what you do. And when you can't, then own it and give solid reasons, not excuses.

2. *Be a coach.* Coaches invite others to the table, looking for their thoughts, ideas, and input. In any team environment, there is a balancing act. The goal isn't to please everyone but to do what is best for the team.

3. *Listen actively.* You might have all kinds of things running through your mind, but when you are with your team, you owe it to them to be "present in the moment" and hear what they are saying. To listen actively, you need to focus on the person speaking. You can also rephrase what the person said, to ensure that you—and the rest of the team—have truly heard what was said. Be careful of being fidgety, preoccupied, or glancing at your phone. Instead, focus on the person by

---

16   Lolly Daskal, "10 Ways You Can Make an Impressive Impact at Work," *Inc.*, April 16, 2018, https://www.inc.com/lolly-daskal/10-ways-you-can-make-an-impressive-impact-at-work.html.

turning your body toward them, maintaining eye contact, and taking in their words.

4. *Stay curious.* The great thing about having a team is hearing different ideas and perspectives. To stay curious, you have to ditch the been-there-done-that attitude by inviting people to share their input and let them know you will take what the team is saying into consideration.

5. *Grow your team members.* You can't be a master of everything. So challenge your team to take on new assignments, to come up with fresh ideas, and to go where they have never gone before.

Organizational

Now you are looking at the big picture and how you can impact the organization as a whole. Consider the following ways to get—and keep—your seat at the leadership table:

1. *Go the extra mile.* When you take the initiative to take on tasks and accomplish goals without being asked, you are going the extra mile. When you offer an act of kindness, you are going the extra mile. When you give credit where credit is due, you are going the extra mile. The point is, whenever you go the extra mile, you will have an impact on your organization. Whenever you do more than what is expected or required, others will take note and, most likely, follow your lead, which ultimately will have a positive impact on your organization. This is called "the ripple effect."

2. *Be a servant leader.* In today's world, you want to lead by serving others. Servant leadership will give your organization

confidence in your abilities, and you will stand out. Your organization will have confidence in you, because it will be evident to all that you don't have a self-motivating agenda. So look for ways to serve and help others. Coming up with ideas and solutions and sharing them in constructive, this-is-how-it-benefits-everyone ways will earn you the respect of everyone around you.

3. *Connect.* To impact your organization, you want to connect and network with those inside your extended organization. You might meet someone who can assist you now, and in the future, and you can reciprocate. Having an organizational impact starts with building relationships, so be willing to connect when the opportunity presents itself.

> **Stay a step ahead by getting into the habit of looking for solutions.**

4. *Be forward thinking.* This relates back to the "What if?" strategy. Stay a step ahead by getting into the habit of looking for solutions. A forward-thinking person is an asset to any organization.

Prepare for Impact

I'm sure you're familiar with the expression, "Is your glass half-empty of half-full?" It's a proverbial phrase, often used rhetorically to illustrate that a situation could be viewed as pessimistic (half-empty) or optimistic (half-full). It's simply a way to determine how we see the world.

I hope you hear me on this: those who tend to be pessimistic are not "bad" people, and those who tend to be optimistic are not "good" people. There are advantages and disadvantages to having either mindset.

Glass-half-full people are solution focused and believe there is always a way to fix a problem. They are the sun-is-always-shining types of people and have a positive outlook on life. However, they can also be stubborn and never accept the fact that something simply can't or won't happen.

Glass-half-empty people are those who focus on roadblocks, hindrances, and the downside of what *might* happen. They balance out the glass-half-full eternal optimists by pointing out realities that need to be considered and/or accounted for.

Certainly, if you want to be a person of impact, then you must lean toward having a glass-half-full mindset. But you must also be open to hearing the negative or downside, so that you consider all possibilities and don't get blindsided.

How do you know which type of person you are? Here are two simple questions to ask yourself:

- Do I dwell on the negative?

- Or do I find the silver lining, even when negative situations occur?

I recently had a conversation with a person in which both of us had similar toxic job experiences. (Perhaps you have been in this type of harmful situation.) We commiserated about the misery of our roles. But we also talked about the positives that resulted from our toxic experiences. My point is that people of impact are realists, but they can always find something positive to learn and to grow from.

It's easy to dwell on the negative. It's much harder to have a positive mindset, one that says you will succeed, despite what your current circumstances tell you. Always remember the following:

> Train your mind to see the negative, and your focus will find the negative.
>
> Train your mind to see the positive, and your focus will find the positive.

Notice I did not say "dismiss," but "train."

***

We have discussed a lot so far! Now it is time to bring it all home in practical ways that will help you make the impact you are looking for.

I suggest choosing three to five ways that you want to impact yourself, your team, and/or your organization. My reason is simple: You don't want to overwhelm yourself by taking on too much. Instead, you want to set yourself up for success. Ideally, you want to choose ways to have an impact that further your success goals, and obviously you can choose the kind of impact you want to have.

The choices you make today will determine where you will be in the future.

As you prepare for impact, the key is to know yourself. Know how you operate. Know your strengths. And yes, know your weaknesses and blind spots. Bring all that information together and make your plan.

Remember that impact catapults you into the spotlight. All eyes are on you, so you have to be prepared to carpe diem: seize the day!

But what do you do when you are unsure of your impact? If you are unsure, that is okay. Take a step back and look at the information you have. Start with your current role, your team, your company.

Then assess where you can have an impact. And never forget: prepare, prepare, prepare. And practice, practice, practice. Over time, practice leads to consistency and confidence, giving you control over the impact you want to make.

As a person of impact, you have the power to choose. And the choices you make today will determine where you will be in the future.

Pull Up Your C.H.A.I.R.— Action Items

As your coach, I want to challenge you to consider the following:

- In your self-reflection journal, write down three to five ways that you are *currently* having an impact on yourself, your team, and your organization.

- What are you unsure of today that you need to gain knowledge and confidence in, so that you can make a greater impact?

- Starting today, what can you do that will make an impact and get you closer to or get you a seat at the leadership table?

"R"—REGRETS

A note to my readers:

You are in the home stretch, and you've got the resolve to finish this book—and apply what you are learning to your life and career.

Now, let's take a step back for a moment then a step forward to understand what regrets you might have over things that have happened in your life, and how *not* to allow them to hold you back.

If you think of the word "regret," I'm sure it conjures up things that you wish had never happened, and feelings of shame and embarrassment may also well up within you.

> **But if you let the negative things in your life hold you back, you will surely miss out on something good.**

But if you let the negative things in your life hold you back, you will surely miss out on something good. Why? Because regret keeps us locked in the past. So what do you do? Here's a simple lesson that can be applied to any regretful situation: What can I learn from it that I can apply going forward? That simple question will turn a negative into a positive, allowing you to keep moving forward. While we've all done things that we've regretted, or had things happen to us that we regret, it is completely within our choosing whether or not we collapse under the weight of regret or use it to empower and catapult us to new heights!

CHAPTER

13

YOU MISS 100 PERCENT OF THE SHOTS YOU DON'T TAKE

NO REGRETS

If not us, then who? If not now, then when?
—JOHN LEWIS

Regret. It's a tiny word, only six letters long, that has so much power. So much impact. So much control. Regret is distressful to the mind, filling us with sorrow over what has happened or not happened, what has been done or failed to have been done, or what has been said or not said. And I have a personal mission to eliminate its power. Negate its impact. Take away its control.

How do I do this?

By living out my personal mantra: no regrets.

You may wonder why I chose "no regrets" as a mantra to live my life by.

I was born with sickle cell anemia but wasn't diagnosed until I was a young girl. Sadly, once I was diagnosed, the doctors told me all the things I *couldn't* and *shouldn't* do: I couldn't go swimming because the cold water can exacerbate the illness. I couldn't play baseball because I might get hurt, which would worsen the disease. I had to avoid any kind of stressful situation, because stress is like adding gasoline to a fire—it would make the disease become unmanageable. I had to come to grips with the fact that I had a debilitating, life-threatening disease.

I was told to sit out my life and watch from the sidelines.

When I was eight years old, I decided I wanted to be a lawyer, and my parents were fully supportive, even though there were no lawyers or "legal" people in our family. I envisioned myself as the first African American female Supreme Court justice and thought that being a lawyer would get me there. In the years following, I planned my entire "lawyer" path through high school and college by engaging in groups that exposed me to public speaking, debates, etc., so that I would be comfortable being in the public limelight.

Fast-forward to 1998. I had just finished a two-year break from school, after graduating from Lipscomb University with a bachelor of arts degree in political science. (In those two years, I traveled around the country representing Lipscomb as an admissions director.) I was thinking about going to Nashville School of Law, until law school recruiters started showing up at Lipscomb, and one of the universities represented was Pepperdine Caruso School of Law. After meeting with the recruiter, Steve Potts, I fell in love with Pepperdine, and I was set on going there.

The problem? My LSAT scores were not good, and I had never been a great standardized test taker. However, when I told Steve that my scores weren't good enough, he encouraged me to apply anyway. I thought, *Why not? Nothing ventured, nothing gained.* Because of what my parents had instilled in me about how to face obstacles, I decided that I didn't want to look back and regret not trying for admittance to Pepperdine.

Then, one day in June 1998, I got a call from Steve. He said, "Are you sitting down?"

I thought, *Man, he's going to reject me.*

"I know you expressed concern about your grades," said Steve, "but I have good news for you ... congratulations, you've been admitted to Pepperdine law school, and we are giving you conditional admittance. You'll have to check in regularly with your advisor, and there will be some provisions during your first semester. However, if you demonstrate that you belong here, that you can do well, then the conditions will be dropped."

At the end of the phone call, I dropped to my knees with tears in my eyes and thanked God for making my dreams come true.

I was so excited to call my parents with this great news. However, when I told them that I was moving to Malibu, California, my dad thought I was crazy. Having been stationed as a Marine in San Diego, he hated California. My mom also said there was no way they could afford to send me to Pepperdine.

At that point, I could have been deflated. I could have simply given up.

But I didn't. I decided to make my way—to chart my own course.

The next day I called the admissions office and told them of my financial dilemma … and they were fantastic! I called so much that I'm sure they knew my name and phone number by heart, and they helped me apply for every scholarship and every grant possible. I was responsible for room and board, but the rest would be covered by scholarships and grants.

In August 1998, I loaded up my red Chevy Berretta, kissed my parents goodbye, and drove thirty-six hours from Tennessee to Malibu, with my Rand McNally paper map and my CD player.

I couldn't contain my excitement. Arriving at Pepperdine Caruso School of Law was a dream come true.

The first year of law school was one of the hardest experiences I had faced. During the first semester, I started having debilitating chest pains—the "I dropped to my knees, because I couldn't breathe" kind of chest pains.

At Christmas, we went to see a doctor. He said, "You know what's causing your chest pains. It's your sickle cell. Your body can't handle the stress. It's law school or your health."

All my life, people have told me what I can't and shouldn't do. "Sit on the sidelines," they said. "You are not like everyone else," they said.

And here I was again being told how dangerous it was, how harmful it was, why I should sit out my life *again*!

They are deciding my future, I thought. Ugh, this always happens. A conversation about me without me.

Well, not this time.

I literally dragged my chair up to this conversation. "I have something to say about my future and what happens to me right here and right now."

I have to say what I have to say.

I looked at my mother. "Mom, I have wanted to be a lawyer since I was eight. If I quit now, I will regret it for the rest of my life."

Until I spoke up, I was going to be left out of one of the most important decisions of my life.

That moment, that experience, is where my mantra of living life with "no regrets" began. I realized that if I don't speak up for myself, no one will do it for me. It is up to me to step into my own power.

The Problem with Regret

The word "regret" conjures up all kinds of negative thoughts: I missed out. I failed. I'm a loser. I'll never try that again. I'm sure you've had these types of thoughts anytime you've regretted something.

The problem with regret is that it's based on comparing something that has happened to a scenario that you *wished* had happened. You've made a choice based on your best decision-making, but the result hasn't turned out the way you wanted it to. But wishful thinking is just that—wishful—and wishful thinking won't get you anywhere; it will keep you stuck right where you are.

Wishful thinking won't get you anywhere.

Another problem with regret is that it chains you to the past and paralyzes you from moving forward. For example, you may have approached your boss about working on a different project, or perhaps you've asked your manager for a raise. You've planned for any resistance, and you've prepared to advocate on your own behalf. But you were told no after hearing various reasons why you can't have what you've asked for.

But let's look at this a little closer.

Do you regret hearing the word "no," or do you regret the *feelings* of failure that come up? I would suggest that you regret how you felt more than hearing the word "no."

There's no doubt you have felt disappointment, loss, frustration, and disillusionment.

So I want to challenge you.

Instead of feeling bad about the action you've taken or the words that you've said, I encourage you to view the situation differently. Remind yourself that you took steps to champion yourself and to move forward. You chose to proactively seek the opportunity, so be proud of yourself!

A no is just a no. If you feel regretful, it's because you have assigned that feeling to perceived failure. I have been told no many times. How did I respond? Today's no is tomorrow's yes. So what if you were told no? Maybe your boss was having a bad day; maybe the answer was no for reasons he couldn't control. The reason is not important. What is important is your reaction. Would you rather try and hear no, so that you can try again in the future? Or would you rather feel regretful never asking at all?

Regret tells us "if only." If only I had approached my boss at a different time. If only I had chosen different words. If only … The truth is we cannot change the past, but we can learn from it.

In chapter 10, I talked about "limiting beliefs." When you live in regret, you are being held hostage by a limiting belief (i.e., *I should have acted on that opportunity*).

Think about a time when an opportunity arose, and you decided not to pursue it. A coworker pursues the opportunity and receives it—

maybe it is a new role, a promotion, a lead on a new project. Secretly, you kick yourself wondering what would have happened if you'd pursued the same opportunity. Your regret can paralyze you, or you can learn from the experience and decide never to miss an opportunity again.

A third problem with regret is that you can take yourself out of the game before you even start. It's sad to say, but I hear people do that all the time. Due to something that has turned out wrong in the past, they decide to "stay in their comfort zone" and "not make waves." Whenever I hear one of my coaching clients express these sentiments, I immediately challenge them to look at what has happened in the past and figure out what they can learn and apply moving forward, which is something you can do as well. I encourage you to be a "What if?" person. What if you actually accomplished what you desperately want? How would that make you feel?"

Think about the following people:[17]

- Thomas Edison was told by his teachers he was "too stupid to learn anything."

- Walt Disney was told by his former newspaper editor that he "lacked imagination and had no good ideas."

- Albert Einstein didn't start speaking until he was four or reading until he was seven, and he was thought to be mentally handicapped.

- J. K. Rowling was a broke, depressed, divorced single mother simultaneously writing a novel while studying.

- Oprah Winfrey was fired from her first TV job as an anchor in Baltimore.

---

17   Sebastian Kipman, "15 Highly Successful People Who Failed on Their Way to Success," Life Hack, March 2, 2021, https://www.lifehack.org/articles/productivity/15-highly-successful-people-who-failed-their-way-success.html.

Each of these people has had incredible success. But what if they'd never followed their dreams? What if they'd allowed the negative comments from others or their sad circumstances to shut them down? And what if someone else did what Edison, Disney, Einstein, Rowling, or Winfrey had in their hearts to do? They all would have missed 100 percent of the shots they didn't take and would have lived with regret. However, knowing they had great dreams inside of them, they were determined to live up to their potential. They championed themselves when no one else would, and they fulfilled their destinies.

> **Be the person who won't settle for less than what they were destined for, and how they were designed to be.**

Don't be like the majority of people who let what is in their hearts die within them. I'll guarantee you they are living lives of regret. Instead, be the part of the minority—be the person who won't settle for less than what they were destined for, and how they were designed to be ... and live your life with no regrets.

Regret Should Be a Key Motivator

I get that not everything turns out the way you want it to. I've been in that position countless times, and I'm 100 percent sure that I'll be in it again. But I use regret as a positive motivator, and you can too. For instance, you have already learned several strategies designed to help you champion yourself, to advocate for yourself, and to pull up a chair to the table you want to be at. What are you going to do with these strategies? Are you going to say, "They are really great!" Then, the next time you have an opportunity to champion yourself, you take the easy way out and say no to the opportunity, and regret it later? Or are you willing to do the work, so that you don't miss opportunities going forward? Are you going to commit to yourself that you are going to invest in yourself—starting today—so that you don't have any regrets about an opportunity missed or a path you didn't take?

People often don't take action because of fear—fear of failure, fear of what someone might or might not say, fear of not getting what they want … the list of fears is endless. Fear causes us to hesitate. It causes reluctance.

But I want you to think about something:

> When you don't take action, how often do you regret it?
> When you don't take a chance, how often do you regret it?
> When you don't do something you really want to do, how often do you regret it?

I'm sure that particular memories came to mind when you thought about those questions. But you always have a choice: you can choose to let regret hold you hostage to the past, or you can choose to use regret as a key motivator to accomplish your goals, to pursue success, and to make your dreams a reality.

Using Regret to Your Advantage

The main reason you regret something is that you feel it is lost forever. But you need to ask yourselves, "Is X or Y really lost forever?" Or have you suffered a temporary setback? Will you see the situation as a learning curve, or will you fall by the side of the road and give up?

Most people would say that regret causes them to look backward, to look at things that have happened in the past that have caused them some level of emotional pain, and say, "I'll never do that again." However, I want to give you a different perspective: use regret to cause you to look forward. How? When you look back at something you regret, figure out exactly *what* you regret and promise yourself *not* to do the same thing in the future. Tell yourself that the next time X or Y happens, you won't regret your reaction. That's how you use regret to your advantage.

Do you want to know my secret to living a life of no regrets?

It's simple.

Every day, in any situation where I need to make a decision, I ask myself one question: "Will I regret it?"

- I want a promotion. If I don't ask, will I regret it?

- I want a new role or a new job. If I don't ask, will I regret it?

- I want to share an idea. If I don't say something, will I regret it?

- Someone presents an opportunity that I have never considered. If I don't take this chance now, will I regret it?

If the answer is yes to these types of questions, then guess what? The decision has been made for me, because I don't live with regret. The question about regret has helped me pivot and transition whenever I've needed to. It has helped me decide when to move forward. When people ask me how I have done X or Y in my career, especially in the cutthroat arena of politics, making decisions based on "no regrets" is my standard answer.

Having no regrets is how I take chances—well-thought-out chances. I know what I'm doing, even if I don't know all the variables, and I don't want to see someone else doing what I wanted to do and wonder why I didn't try.

Whenever you chart a new course or try something new, you are going to have doubt. You are going to feel anxious. The unknown will do that to you. But think about this: If you are putting the strategies into place that we've discussed, then why not do what you want to do … the only thing you have to lose is the feeling of regret!

Here's a great list of fifteen things that people who have no regrets *don't* do:[18]

1. They don't give up.

2. They don't avoid talking about things.

3. They don't stay home.

4. They don't wait for others to do something.

5. They don't strive for perfection.

6. They don't get caught up in drama.

7. They don't avoid telling the truth.

8. They don't ignore their responsibilities.

9. They don't stress out.

10. They don't skimp on their health.

11. They don't avoid people.

12. They don't envy others.

13. They don't forget the simple pleasures in life.

14. They don't stray from their moral compass.

15. They don't say no too often.

---

18   Maggie Heath, "15 Things People Who Have No Regrets Don't Do," Life Hack, accessed September 2021, https://www.lifehack.org/articles/communication/15-things-people-who-have-regrets-dont.html.

"Will I regret it?" I'm sure you can see the power of that question, and I wholeheartedly encourage you to adopt this question into your life! Use "regret" to your advantage, and you won't miss opportunities that are presented to you.

You only have one life to live ... choose a life of no regrets.

Pull Up Your C.H.A.I.R.— Action Items

As your coach, I want to challenge you to consider the following:

- When you hear the word "no," how can you change it from a negative to a positive?

- When you think of the word "regret," what feelings come to mind?

- On the list of fifteen things that people who have no regrets *don't* do, which can you identify with?

- Are you ready and willing to make "no regrets" a life mantra?

CHAPTER

14

I SAID YES

HOW TO AVOID REGRETS

Fear is temporary. Regret is forever.
—*ANONYMOUS*

Here's a truth: fear can be paralyzing, but fear can also be a galvanizing force to take action.

In 2018, fear and uncertainty dominated most of my year. I lost my job in May 2018. Frankly, it was time for me to leave that role … actually it was past time. I had accomplished what I wanted regarding my professional growth, and I'm a big believer in knowing what you want to get out of any job and how it is going to benefit you. In addition to accomplishing my personal and professional goals, I was proud of the accomplishments we achieved as a team.

At this point, I was mentally and physically exhausted. I'd spent years traveling and kept a grueling schedule, and at different points in my career I had traveled eight months of the year.

Coincidentally, the day I lost my job, I had a meeting about my next role. The person I met with was a friend I met on Capitol Hill in 2003. We had accomplished major initiatives on behalf of the congressmen we served and have been friends ever since. He was and remains at the top of my list of people I tremendously respect.

I recounted the events of the morning to him.

He asked, "Have you ever taken a break in your career?"

"No," I replied.

Why would I do that? I am one of those people who ends a job on Friday and begins a new job on Monday.

He responded, "Take some time off. I don't know whether that's a few weeks or a few months. But my advice is, you need a break."

The timing of this conversation provided much-needed perspective.

He was right. I needed a break. For the rest of May and June, I did nothing but sleep and relax. I woke up, ate, watched TV, and went back to sleep. After a few weeks of rest, I went back home to Tennessee to help a close friend who was running for Congress. When you believe in your candidate, there is nothing better than being on the campaign trail advocating for that person!

True to form, by August, my dad started asking about what I was going to do next and when I was going back to work. I told him not to worry about it. He told me it was time to figure it out.

In August, I went back to DC to contemplate my next steps.

Launching my own lobbying firm has always been an interesting idea to me. Over the years, various people asked if I had thought about starting my own firm.

The easy path was to apply for lobbying and government affairs jobs, basically the same job I just left. I interviewed with a couple of companies who were interested in hiring me. But I kept coming back to the same question: "Why would I continue to work for anyone else?" My answer: "If I am going to stay in Washington, I should work for myself." But there was one problem: I had no clue how to start a business. Actually, there was a second problem: I didn't have any potential clients.

I prayed about my next move while I continued to interview for jobs.

In October, I finally asked the deciding question: "If I go to work for another organization, will I regret it?" The answer was a resounding yes! I just wasn't excited about going to work for another organization, large or small. I was tired of office politics and the corresponding drama.

Okay, great ... decision made!

Now came the hard part—"How do I start a lobbying firm?"

Needless to say, I rolled up my sleeves and got to work. Meanwhile, my parents were concerned and kept asking, "Do you know what you are doing?"

I said no, but that I would figure it out.

My brother told me to go for it and reminded my parents that I had figured out how to have a successful career in Washington, and I would figure this out too. This meant starting from scratch—determining the type of business I wanted (LLC, S corp., etc.), a business name, a business bank account, website, logo, business cards, and more.

Three years later, I can tell you that starting a firm was one of the best decisions I have ever made. It has been scary with lots of uncertainty, but I absolutely love it! I don't dread the next email anymore or the next call from my boss. I wake up happy every single morning, and I'm thrilled for the opportunity to represent amazing clients.

If It's Got to Be, It's Up to Me

In the political and business circles I work in, I often hear things like, "That person doesn't have the experience but got that job," and "That person hasn't been here long enough but got that opportunity," and "Why did they choose that person for the role, when they could have chosen someone else?"

I'm sure you've heard similar questions.

What separates those who get the opportunities from those who don't? Often, it comes down to who is willing to take a chance to champion themselves versus those who aren't willing to raise their hand on their own behalf. Those who are willing have no regrets. They would rather hear no than not try at all. They have the courage to try something new.

The question is, Do you have that same type of courage?

When you're faced with a decision or an opportunity, ask yourself, "What am I afraid of? What's the worst that can happen? Someone might say no? Perhaps I'll be embarrassed for a few moments?"

Who cares?

What would you regret, if you didn't take the chance?

The answer to those questions is why I love the refrain, "If it's got to be, it's up to me." I'm sure you've found out in life that no one is going to make decisions for you, and I encourage you to adopt the above saying for your own life. Here is one way it has played out in my life.

What would you regret, if you didn't get the chance?

If you recall, in the introduction I told you about an experience I had early in my political career. I had volunteered for a congressional campaign, and we had no idea if we were going to win. But on election night, November 2002, my boss won by a point. When I told my parents that the congressman-elect asked me to go to Washington with him, my dad thought I was crazy—it was only a year after 9/11.

However, my mom simply said, "You will regret it if you don't try."

A month later, the day after Christmas 2002, I moved to Washington, DC. I never envisioned I would be in the city that is the center of the free world, working with presidents, Congress, and elected officials. But when the opportunity presented itself, I said yes. I told myself I would try it for a few months, and if I didn't like it, I would move back to Tennessee. I would at least try. In other words, "If it's got to be, it's up to me."

Throughout this book, you have read my stories—and stories from others—about new opportunities and new jobs in which I had no idea how to do the work; however, I never let fear and regret control my decisions. I can tell you that I've made decision after decision after decision—personal and professional—knowing that if I didn't take a chance, I would regret it.

Avoiding regret can stir your heart to take positive action, if you are willing to be courageous and take a chance. So get comfortable being uncomfortable.

Get comfortable being uncomfortable.

As you look at your life, you have choices before you. Will you choose fear and certain regret? Or opportunity and potential success?

Pull Up Your C.H.A.I.R.— Action Items

As your coach, I want to challenge you to consider the following:

- Reflect on people you've known who have made a particular decision or decided to forgo one. Would you have made the same decision? Why or why not?

- How can you get comfortable with the uncomfortable in your current situation?

- What decisions have you made that other people thought you were crazy for making but turned out well for you?

- How does the refrain, "If it's got to be, it's up to me" apply to your life?

CHAPTER

15

FOR THE REST OF MY LIFE

THE ROAD AHEAD

If we wait until we are ready, we'll be waiting the rest of our lives.
—LEMONY SNICKET

By now, you probably think I'm a crazy risk taker. Actually, I'm very conservative by nature. I just refuse to sit around and watch others do what I know I can do myself.

This mentality is what led me to start a coaching business.

Earlier in this book, I mentioned that I gave a speech in Nashville on March 12, 2020, to a group of executives from various industries, days before the country shut down due to the pandemic. I met some amazing people at that meeting with whom I've stayed in touch.

On Easter morning 2020, my father passed away suddenly. His heart stopped. My world shattered. Almost a year and a half later, I still can't believe he is gone. The love, discipline, work ethic, drive, and determination he taught my brother and me fuel us to this day.

In the weeks following, I kept reflecting on the many lessons he taught me. He was my harshest critic, while also expressing how proud he was of me. I truly am my father's daughter. Marines are motivated and challenged by criticism, and my father used the same tactics on me. He pushed me to be the best, and if I did my best, the result didn't matter. I decided I was going to work my butt off to make him proud. He may be gone, but he would expect nothing less.

That summer, I was contacted by a coaching company, asking if I wanted to coach CEOs. I was flattered by the outreach, but I decided not to pursue it. The structure of the program was time consuming and wouldn't fit with my lobbying business.

I thanked the gentleman for the calls and moved on.

By August, I realized this pandemic was going to last awhile. I knew that I couldn't sit around for months with nothing to show for this downtime. So I challenged myself. If I didn't use this time to further my business and my professional growth, it would be opportunity missed and time wasted. I couldn't come out of the pandemic with nothing to show for my time.

A few weeks later, in the sad wake of George Floyd's murder, my alma mater, Pepperdine Caruso School of Law, asked me to be on a panel and speak about my experiences with race in the workplace. One of the audience members asked each of us about a lesson we have learned in our career. When my turn came, I responded, "As I reflect on my professional experiences with race and ageism, I now realize I need to reach back to help others."

After the panel, I decided to relaunch my public speaking career. I love public speaking and have given countless speeches throughout my career. I soon found a speakers group called The Speaker Lab and joined immediately. I also decided to formally launch my C.H.A.I.R. Leader-

> **I now realize I need to reach back to help others.**

ship program, using one strategy for each letter of Congresswoman Chisholm's "chair" quote that I have used to excel in my career.

Once I started public speaking, people would approach me after a speech and ask how I excelled in my career, how had I achieved the leadership roles in which I had served? I now had an answer for that question: "I excelled using the C.H.A.I.R. model. No one invited me to the table; I brought my own chair and made my own way."

The call about coaching CEOs stuck with me. Also, attendees who'd heard me speak in Nashville months earlier asked if I had considered coaching individuals. Now I was intrigued. "What do others see in me that makes them think I could coach others?"

I started to give the idea of leadership and professional coaching serious thought. I loved mentoring individuals, but did I have what it takes to be a coach?

After days of prayer and serious thought, I started my coaching business with a mission to coach and help others on their professional journeys. I learned through trial and error; no one guided my journey. But I wanted to help others achieve and succeed in their career journey, without the guesswork I went through.

"Can I really do this?" I asked myself.

Yes, I can!

And I would have no regrets.

Days later, a lady randomly sent me a private chat on Zoom, offering to connect me to a social media business coach who could help me figure out how to structure and launch my coaching program.

At the end of my consultation call, he asked, "Are you ready to get started?"

I said *yes!*

"I am ready to start immediately."

I am incredibly grateful to both individuals for helping me launch the C.H.A.I.R. Leadership program. My social media business coach taught me how to launch an online course and how to attract coaching clients online. Because of the lessons he taught, one day I received a message on LinkedIn from someone I didn't know, asking if I was interested in writing a book.

I said *yes!*

Who doesn't dream about writing a book someday?

That *yes* led to a book deal and podcast, a TEDx talk, and growing my leadership program to a monthly mastermind program.

You never know what is on the other side of *yes!* Trust me on this.

Fight or Flight

I'm sure you've heard of the expression "fight or flight." The fight-or-flight response is hardwired within the amygdala, which is a collection of cells near the base of the brain and is involved in our behavioral and emotional response. It controls our physiological reaction to something that is real or perceived as mentally or physically terrifying. The fight-or-flight response is triggered by the release of hormones that prepare us either to stay and deal with a threat or to run away to safety.

With the fight-or-flight response in mind, I want you to think about asking your boss for a raise. Or approaching your manager for a new project. Or perhaps looking for a new job at a different company. Each of these examples can cause you to be anxious or even fearful. But here's the bottom line: if you let anxiety or fear control your decisions, you will always choose flight. In other words, you won't ask for the raise. You'll shy away from that new project. You'll choose the status quo regarding your job. And the "What ifs?" and regrets will haunt you.

So I have another approach for you.

Repeat after me: "I said yes."

Say that several times out loud.

How does it feel to say, "I said *yes*"? I said yes to asking my boss for a raise. I said yes to approaching my manager for a new project. I said yes to looking for a new job at a different company.

I'll bet it feels pretty good.

So the next time you have an opportunity, the next time you are sitting in a meeting, knowing you have a valuable contribution to add, you can either say

> **Every day is a new day to say yes.**

nothing and live with the regret ... or, at the end of the meeting, you can pat yourself on the back for saying yes while walking out the door with a spring in your step.

Every day is a new day to show up differently. Every day is a new day to say yes. Every day is a new day to use past regrets to your advantage and create new opportunities. I often call this the "risk management way to manage your career."

No doubt you have heard the phrase "risk versus reward." It is mostly used in financial arenas. Risk versus reward, according to the *Cambridge Dictionary*, is "the possible profit that a particular activity may make, in relation to the risk involved in doing it." From this point on in your life, I encourage you to think of your decisions in terms of risk versus reward. Ask yourself, "What am I risking?" Actually, here's a better question: "What reward is waiting for me?"

The truth is, if you want rewards in life, you have to take risks. And if you are willing to focus on the rewards, you will avoid making excuses. Instead, you will do the work necessary. You will champion yourself. You will pull up a chair to the table, even if you weren't invited.

To remind yourself to focus on rewards, here are a couple of mantras you can put on sticky notes, write out in your self-reflection journal, or even have a plaque created:

We only regret the chances we didn't take. Will you practice until you overcome regrets? Appreciate everything; regret nothing.

Over the years, I've said yes to overcoming the debilitation of sickle cell anemia, leading the restaurant industry into new territory, directing a newly created political team as a political newbie, moving from a small rural town to the metropolis of Washington, DC, and starting a coaching and consulting business.

I've also said yes to

- being a first-generation college student;

- working on a factory assembly line to learn the value of going to school and furthering my education;

- being the kid who didn't belong in law school, yet receiving the highest honor bestowed to a third-year Pepperdine law student;

- leading a death penalty case in my first summer job in the legal field;

- serving on and chairing corporate and nonprofit boards; and

- working with four presidential administrations.

When you think about it, life comes down to a series of choices—choices we make on a daily basis that affect our entire lives. Here are three that are completely within our control:

- Speaking up or staying silent

- Putting up our hand or sitting on it

- Saying yes or living with regret

With these choices in mind, how important is it to hear yourself say, "I said *yes*"?

Saying yes was so important to award-winning creator, producer, and writer Shonda Rhimes that she spent a year doing just that, saying yes, and credits this decision with changing her life. She also wrote a best-selling book titled *Year of the Yes*.

Forbes magazine contributor Amy Blaschka wrote an article on the writer-producer and notes that Rhimes's *year of saying yes* started when her sister said to her at a family Thanksgiving dinner, "You never say yes to anything."[19]

In a moving TED Talk on the topic, Rhimes says, "Anything that made me nervous, took me out of my comfort zone, I forced myself to say yes to. And a crazy thing happened: the very act of doing the thing that scared me undid the fear, made it not scary. My fear of

---

19   Amy Blaschka, "Five Reasons Why Saying 'Yes' Is the Best Decision for Your Career," *Forbes*, November 21, 2019, https://www.forbes.com/sites/amy-blaschka/2019/11/21/five-reasons-why-saying-yes-is-the-best-decision-for-your-career/?sh=29c964352184.

public speaking, my social anxiety, poof, gone. It's amazing, the power of one word."[20]

In her article, Blaschka lists five reasons why saying yes is best for your career:[21]

1. Saying yes opens you up to new challenges and opportunities.

2. Saying yes invites collaboration.

3. Saying yes empowers and affirms others.

4. Saying yes creates an environment where it's safe to try, fail, learn, and innovate.

5. Saying yes makes life more fun.

Never forget that the word "yes" is your most powerful ally. And when "I said *yes*" becomes part of who you are, you will build bridges, you will open doors, and you will live with fulfillment instead of regret.

When "I said *yes*" becomes part of your vocabulary, you will be giving yourself permission to do your best, and if something doesn't turn out the way you want it to, you will have learned something new about yourself or perhaps a different way to approach the outcome you desire. While saying yes can cause some anxious moments, once you get past your initial emotions, you'll be surprised at the possibilities you see, and the outside-the-box thinking that occupies your thoughts.

In closing, I want to ask you this: Are you ready to roll up your sleeves? To do the work necessary? Are you willing to trust yourself? Are you ready to make "I said *yes*" part of your daily mindset?

---

20 Amy Blaschka, "Five Reasons Why Saying 'Yes' Is the Best Decision for Your Career," Shonda Rhimes, "My Year of Saying Yes to Everything," TED Talk, 2016, 18:35, https://www.ted.com/talks/shonda_rhimes_my_year_of_saying_yes_to_everything.

21 Amy Blaschka, "Five Reasons Why Saying 'Yes' Is the Best Decision for Your Career," Shonda Rhimes, "My Year of Saying Yes to Everything."

Pull Up Your C.H.A.I.R.— Action Items

As your coach, I want to challenge you to consider the following:

- What can you say *yes* to today?

- Who can you say *yes* to today?

- How can you say *yes* to yourself today?

- In what ways will saying *yes* change your life, in the short and long term?

AFTERWORD

Don't let someone dim your light just because it's shining in their eyes.
—*C. CONSTANTINIDES*

As we draw to the close of this book, I hope you enjoyed the stories and lessons. I hope you marked the pages, followed the exercises, and are ready to implement these strategies in your personal and professional life.

Most of all, I hope you are ready to say *yes* to yourself. To step into your power. To find your voice and decide it is time to not only pull up your chair to the table but set the table as well.

That is what this book and these five C.H.A.I.R. strategies are all about—believing in yourself and putting yourself at the top of your to-do list.

> **I hope you are ready to say *yes* to yourself.**

Remember:

C—champion yourself
H—honesty
A—adaptability
I—impact
R—regrets

I've followed these five strategies on the path to success, and you can too.

My family instilled in me the belief that I could do anything I wanted to do, be anything I wanted to be. They have been and continue to be my coaches.

Perhaps you don't have anyone as your coach and encourager … well, you do now: me.

I've faced many obstacles and much adversity in my life and still do. I could have used my health as an excuse, but I didn't. I still have serious health challenges to this day, but that doesn't stop me. If anything, these challenges provide a sense of urgency to do more, to achieve more, while I can.

I was told to sit out my life. That I couldn't be like everyone else. I was always going to be the underdog. But I overcame the naysayers and their perceived obstacles.

That is why this book is called *Pull Up Your C.H.A.I.R.* I wasn't about to live my life sitting on the sidelines. I showed up every day, ready to contribute, ready to learn, ready to do what I needed to do to get where I wanted to go. If I can do it, you can too.

If I can show up differently, then you can too. I am not going to allow you to sit on the sidelines without understanding and getting in touch with your full potential.

It's time.

Decide today that you are going to step forward, bring your own chair to your life, to your work, to your accomplishments.

Stop sitting it out at work. Stop sitting out your life. It's not enough.

As your coach, I see you. I know you. I have been you. I believe in you and your potential to achieve all that your heart desires—in business and in life.

If you truly want to step into your power and potential, ask yourself these every day:

1. "Am I going to just survive, or will I thrive?"

2. "How will I show up differently?"

Each day is a gift. There are no good days or bad days.

Only *you* can decide that you are ready to thrive and show up differently.

Only *you* can choose to pull up your chair and create the conversations that are going to change your career and your life.

Only *you* can decide to do nothing.

Now ask yourself: "Which path will I choose?"

ABOUT CICELY SIMPSON

Cicely Simpson is a nationally known public speaker, leadership coach, author, and entrepreneur as the founder and CEO of Summit Public Affairs.

C.H.A.I.R. Leadership is Cicely's proprietary leadership program. In this program, she coaches clients on how to pull up their chair in business and in life. She developed the program based on five strategies—one for each letter of the word "C.H.A.I.R." inspired by the famous quote from Shirley Chisholm, the first African American congresswoman.

Cicely has successfully navigated the intersection of business and politics for the last twenty-five years, serving in the following roles:

- Founder and CEO, Summit Public Affairs, a bipartisan government affairs and communications firm.

- Executive vice president of public affairs at the National Restaurant Association, leading the restaurant industry's public affairs strategy at all levels of government to achieve the industry's public policy and political goals.

- Vice president of government affairs at Dunkin' Brands Inc., the franchisor and corporate parent of Dunkin' Donuts and Baskin-Robbins restaurants; Cicely led the company's legislative, regulatory, and political strategy with federal, state, local, and international governments.

- Legislative director for two Tennessee congressmen, US Rep. Jim Cooper and US Rep. Lincoln Davis, on Capitol Hill in Washington, DC.

- Law firm of Lewis, King, Krieg & Waldrop in Nashville.

- Tennessee Attorney General's Criminal Division.

Cicely has received numerous awards and recognition for her leadership in these and other roles:

- Nation's Restaurant News "Top 10 Power List"

- *The Hill's* "Top Lobbyists" of 2015, 2016, and 2017

- Association Trends 2016: Leading Association Lobbyists award

- African American Leadership in Food Service and Hospitality

Cicely received a juris doctor from Pepperdine Caruso School of Law and a bachelor of arts degree in political science from Lipscomb University.

Leveraging her experience in business, public policy, politics, and legal affairs, she possesses a wealth of leadership experience and knowledge to guide clients who seek to pull up their chair and set their table of success.

For more information about Cicely and her coaching and training programs, including a *free* one-minute leadership quiz, go to https://www.cicelysimpson.com.

Cicely Simpson